Our VANISHING LANDSCAPE

Our VANISHING LANDSCAPE

by ERIC SLOANE

BALLANTINE BOOKS • NEW YORK

Library of Congress Catalog Card Number: 55-12078
ISBN 0-345-33216-4

This edition published by arrangement with
Funk & Wagnalls, Inc.

Manufactured in the United States of America

First Ballantine Books Edition: December 1974

9 8 7 6 5 4

Author's Note

THE PATTERN of our early landscape was capacious and orderly. Its texture, which were the people and their farms, had the mellowness and dignity of well-seasoned wood. Close at hand there were lanes with vaulting canopies of trees and among them were houses with personalities like human beings. At a distance it was all like a patchwork quilt of farm plots sewn together with a rough black stitching of stone fences.

But the advance of "improvements" has done blatant and rude things to much of this inherited landscape. It began with billboards and roadside stands, soon to be followed by bungalows to match. We thought these things were forgivable indications of a growing countryside and that, so far from becoming typical American scenery, they would soon rot and disappear. But this pattern of organized confusion quickly led to sewers and paved streets. Supermarkets and shopping centers appeared, flanked by homes that looked like more supermarkets and shopping centers. The few remaining scenes with vaulting canopies of trees and houses with personalities like human beings, soon looked uncomfortable and apologetic.

In America there are still a few quiet white villages and people who feel protected by their town's inherent taste and its persistence to stay as it was. There are still those who motor out to the villages with the belief that these landmarks will always remain. But they are both wrong; the growing changes rung on the landscape of today are the Americana of tomorrow.

7

There have been admirable volumes of photographic reverence for early American landscape, but they are usually accompanied by a nostalgic evoking of the past which indicates that to accept any taste of yesteryear would be masquerading in Colonial costume. Restorations, too, often put the brand of "curious and obsolete" on early design. Some people can pass by an enchanting architectural relic without even noticing it. Paint 1792 over the front door and it at once becomes a notable landmark to them.

One "restored Early American village" in New England displays treasures of primitive design, but the exhibit also includes a building with the bones of a prehistoric mastodon. It is like the modern parent who says, "In the old days, children were extremely polite"; so the child is led to believe that good manners are something of an obsolete past.

The general trend of architectural thought today is that a new structure must not look like an old one, else we have not progressed. "Progress," however, must sometimes mark time to let good taste catch up with it whenever the two have not moved in step. In our hunger for improvement, we have unnecessarily changed many things. The concrete superhighway is indicative of rapid progress; equally so is the sad disappearance of the adjacent landscape.

This book which is the sort of thing referred to as a "mirror of the past," will have done its job well only if it first reflects the present, as a mirror really does. When a man has lost sight of his past, he loses his ability to look forward intelligently. With this thought in mind, I hope that my sketches in word and drawing will amount to more than drippy nostalgia.

1857

Asked to name some physical symbol of America, the first thing coming to mind might be the skyscraper. But the tree which once imaged the New World, still symbolizes it more than anything else. Our entire wealth came from the forest, even up until the beginning of the present century. The Iron Age was necessarily a Wood Age too, for our forests were stripped to make charcoal, then the only smelting fuel.

When the romantic era was cluttering parks with statuary, New York was planning a Central Park monument to the American Pioneer. In searching for a subject, Bryant, who was descended from Mayflower Puritans, was consulted. He recalled that the forest was really the backbone of the New World and that "the groves were God's first temples." "Why not plant a tree?" he said. "You could find no more suitable symbol."

You might wonder why modern lumber does not last the way it did in the olden times. What did trees have then that they don't have now? Much has been attributed to "proper seasoning" by "men who knew wood" and who "had all the time in the world." But the old-timers who really had less time than we have now with our time-savers, knew the answer. They were using first-growth timber, something you seldom hear of today. This was wood grown from untouched earth with the humus and peat and natural rot of age-old forests. Its grain was strong and destined to harden with the years rather than to decay. So-called "rotten" first-growth chestnut-siding has been replaced from two-hundred-year-old barns, only to show that, beneath the weathered surface, the wood was still good. In fact it was so hard that the saw-blade burned hot under its flintlike texture. Trees grown from farm-cleared fields are of second or third growth and they have neither the same strength nor longevity.

The oldest farmhouses were usually graced with one big first-growth tree. Often the farm homesite itself was chosen by the location of such a tree. Into that tree went the memories of all the forests of great trees that had disappeared around it. The farmer might have said he left it for shade or to please his wife's decorative sense; more truly it was a deep-felt emblem that tied his efforts to the past, so that he might never forget the time when all pioneer man's needs came from the forest.

As you motor into the American countryside, you will frequently see, along the silhouette of ridges, such a tall tree rising above the rest. Old-timers recognize them as "forest trees" or "first-growth trees"; surveying records call them "markers." They are monuments to the days when the entire forest in that area was cleared away. All farmed land was once barren of trees except for these markers and the few farmhouse giants that remained. "As I stand on the hilltop" reads an account of 1810, "the farms are mosaiced up to the river bank and even through the deepest wrinkles in the anatomy of land. As for the trees, as far as my eye can reach, I can count them on my two hands."

Forests in America were first looked upon as enemies to agriculture. The ax was a weapon instead of a tool. Very few first trees remain but when one is beheld and you can visualize the original countryside covered with such giant growth the effect is almost overwhelming. It was indeed a world beyond present-day comprehension.

In 1850 James Fenimore Cooper wrote, "It is feared that few among the younger generation of trees now springing up will ever attain the dignity of the old-forest trees. Very large portions of these woods are already of a second growth and original forest trees are becoming every year more rare. It is often said as an excuse for leaving none standing, that these trees of old forest growth would not live after their companions have been felled; they miss the protection which one gives to another, and exposed to the winds, would soon fall to the ground. As a general rule, this may be true; but the experiment of leaving a few, might have proved successful."

These lines were written when only a few "forest trees" remained in New England; the impact of their great size and the tragedy of their loss was material for poet and artist. We look in doubt at "exaggerated" trees painted by the artists of the Hudson River School, yet we might well ponder on how true a picture they may have painted.

It is difficult to believe that trees comparing to some of California's Redwoods, existed in the east; but records substantiate this fact. Here is an account from Forestville, New York, written in 1841: "Walnut creek in this town has its name from a black walnut tree, which formerly stood a mile above its mouth, and was 36 feet in circumference at its base, gradually and gracefully tapering 80 feet to the first limb. Its entire height was nearly 200 feet, and it was estimated to contain 150 cords of wood, or 50,-000 feet of inch boards. The bark was a foot thick. The tree was entirely sound when blown down in 1822. The butt, 9 feet in length, was transported

10

to Buffalo, having been excavated, and was there occupied as a grocery store. It was subsequently carried by canal to the Atlantic cities, and, splendidly adorned, was exhibited for money to thousands of admirers."—*Gordon's Gazette*.

Today, a black walnut tree half that size would be considered a giant.

The Stuyvesant Pear Tree 1860

Not long ago there were many celebrated trees in America known almost as well as the persons or events making them famous. Perhaps the best known tree in New York and indeed the oldest fruit tree in America was the Stuyvesant Pear Tree which stood at the northeast corner of Third Avenue and 13th Street in Manhattan. Peter Stuyvesant planted it with his own hands in 1647 and for more than two centuries it lived and bore fruit. It was praised by journalists both here and abroad and poets found it popular material. In his "Address to the Stuyvesant Pear Tree," Henry Webb Dunshee said:

> Fam'd Relic of the Ancient Time, as on thy form I gaze,
> My mind reverts to former scenes, to spirit-stirring days;
> Guarding their sacred memories, as ashes in an urn,
> I muse upon those good old times; and sigh for their return.

In 1867, two wagons collided and broke the trunk of the Stuyvesant Pear Tree, bringing to an end its fruitful life of two hundred and twenty years.

Although we all know Ohio as the Buckeye State, few people know the buckeye tree after which it was named. Yet early European accounts tell of New World adventures in the "Buckeye country." Maine was known as the Pine Tree State before it was Maine, named by England whose scouts claimed the straightest pines for navy masts. Almost any schoolboy of a hundred years ago could reel off the names of trees that each state was famed for.

1957

Missing more than any other tree of the old American landscape, is the native chestnut. Even today, when the only available chestnut is that from long dead trees or from old cut lumber, we accept "wormy chestnut" as a particular prize among woods, wormholes and all. From the beginning, it was a favored wood for barn-building and house-siding. It was a prime producer of tannin, and a bearer of food for man and beast. Thomas Jefferson grafted European varieties of chestnut trees in 1775 and about fifty years later Irenée du Pont de Nemours of Wilmington, Delaware, set out chestnut orchards that resulted in a rich distribution over Delaware, Pennsylvania, and New Jersey.

In 1904, the chestnut blight broke out in New York's Brooklyn Botanical Garden with an importation of some oriental plants and the disease spread concentrically for twenty years, killing surely and completely. The hulks of dead chestnut trees, some of which still stand, are almost frightening in size when you happen upon them among today's second-growth trees.

There are still dead first-growth tree giants standing, some nearby abandoned farmhouses or at intersections where they were originally left as surveyors' markings. Their ability to withstand rot for fifty or more years, even after death, is remarkable to those who realize that the same wood today, even with paint, would show decay in five years. These hulks, mostly elm and an occasional chestnut, are things you will not find in the rural landscape of fifty years hence unless you search in deep forests. But today's artists and photographers have had their satisfaction in portrayals of the symphony of age, wherever an ancient farmhouse and first-growth tree could be found as subjects. Little did they know they were recording things of a vanishing landscape.

FARMS

IN THIS AGE, art and the farm might seem far apart. Yet words like "functional," "basic," and "traditional," that define modern art, also describe America's farms.

Whether it is a skyscraper or an old covered bridge, an oil station or an ancient grist-mill, these patterns of everyday life always reflect American culture. But the philosophy of farming has left the more lasting and profound mark on our national landscape and it has made an enduring cradle for the things we now accept as Americana. There are those modernists who receive the changing landscape as a healthy development, who even find character and functional beauty in gravel-pits and factories and billboards, saying this, too, is art. It is presumptuous for a layman to define art, but we might listen to Ruskin who in one of his Oxford lectures said, "There is nothing I tell you with more earnest desire that you should believe than this; that you will never love art well till you love what she mirrors better." America will always cherish the arts of farm life as mirrored symbols of an inherited philosophy.

In the beginning all civilized America was farms and all Americans were farmers who believed that farmers were the founders of civilization. The lessons that a farm teaches are, after all, not reserved for rural life. The evidences of farm living are more than just calluses. The strong individuality of our forefathers was largely a result of an independence that evolved from their isolated farm existences. Everything in those days came the hard way; work was never finished and the word "holiday" was unknown. In fact the only rest periods were Sundays or "Holy Days," from which comes our present word.

Farm life offers the complete satisfaction of knowing that each day's work has been truly productive, a joy scarce in present times. Yet strangely enough, the early American farmer's greatest satisfaction came not from his daily chores, but in his ability to make provisions for the future and in an awareness of his part in fashioning the nation to come. He equipped his home with far heavier foundations than were necessary. He built his barn to last for centuries and he laid a rail fence to survive ten generations. He built stone walls that have lasted so long that they are now a permanent part of the landscape. None of these things are done now, nor do we often consider doing them.

In 1798, Isaac Weld of Dublin reported of the American farmers, "these people are so certain of their future that they spend a lifetime building barns for future generations." Perhaps one of the great changes in American building and farming philosophy has been the abandonment of the enthusiasm for permanence.

A hundred or more years ago, whether you were a blacksmith, a butcher, a carpenter, a politician, or a banker, you were also a farmer. If you were retired, you were a "gentleman farmer." Even the earliest silk-hatted and powdered-wigged American had gnarled hands that knew the plow and the tricks of building a good stone wall. Before setting out for the day, there were chores to be done that often took as much time as a complete day's work for the average man of today. Taken from the word "chare," chore is an early New England expression that has since become an American word. James Russell Lowell's "Biglow Papers" written in 1848 in Yankee dialect, says:

> I love to start out after night's begun,
> And all the chores about the farm are done.

In England, *chares* were servants' work but *chores* were part of every American's life in the New World.

Early America might have been united by the feeling for independence that our schoolbooks emphasize, but we were also held together by the common bonds of farm life. Nowadays the average man in the street would be at a loss chatting with a statesman: a bootblack would wonder what to talk about with a banker. But a while back, we all would have been farmers, with a great many interests in common. Washington and every member of his first Congress farmed with their own hands. He observed that all America was farms and that all Americans were farmers, "a brotherhood of husbandry which knew neither politics nor class." Benjamin Franklin who was one of our first "city men," whose public affairs necessarily kept him away from agriculture, still felt that farming was a necessary part of common education. He always referred to it as a way of life and a complete philosophy for existence. Even he finally succumbed to "that kind of life which is most agreeable" and bought a farm of three hundred acres. "I think it in duty to my children," he wrote, "to manage that the profits of my farm may balance the loss my income will suffer by my retreat into it." Like all early American farmers, he dedicated his life to the future.

Thumbing through old books and looking at the rustic past, we have good reason to be amazed at the way our forefathers lived, and to be affectionately amused at their crude efforts in comfort and convenience. Ox-yokes, butter-churns, foot-warmers, and such musty paraphernalia of yesterday are too often brought out in reverence by lovers of the past and cooed over by fashionable antiquarians.

On the whole, exhuming dead things is an unwholesome business and modern thought has little room for attic material. Unfortunately, the only recognized relics of yesterday's farmers are obsolete curiosities when the greatest relic, their philosophy of living, is seldom considered. We may decorate our homes with Americana to capture the early farm spirit yet completely ignore the way of life it reflected.

Although we are in a healthy era of attic-cleaning, even the most modern-minded must agree that some of the old things are worth saving. Deep thoughts and sacred memories can sometimes be preserved through symbols which at the moment appear insignificant or out of date. Every half century or so, an industry will undergo a hardy change when even its letterheads and trade marks are modernized, yet an old established business may lose recognition by discarding familiar symbols. One industrialist was urged to re-design the name and trade design of his business. "There isn't any design" the advertising man told him, "that can't be benefited by a periodic stream-lining and change." "I wonder then," the industrialist commented, "why they don't modernize the American flag."

There are still many ancient farms in America but the informal grouping of barns and outbuildings which once made each farmstead look like a tiny community, is missing because obsolete structures have been destroyed. The remaining buildings look stark and alone because they were once one of a rambling group. Even a well-restored farmstead could not wisely keep all the sheds and outbuildings of yesteryear's farm. After the house and the big barn, there was always a smaller barn, a spring house, icehouse, milk house, woodshed, and blacksmith shop. These, with the carriage shed and privy and chicken houses, all made up of a composition of geometric shapes that delighted the eye with its ability to blend with the contours of rolling land. All the old farms "scattered" or "rambled" in this fashion except the

15

Maine and New Hampshire farms which were "jined" or joined into a continuous group of buildings. This "joined architecture" enabled the farmer to do his complete chores during a bad snow, without ever leaving the shelter of his buildings.

The old farms "Rambled" unless they were "Jined"

Connecticut

Maine

There are those who will deny any disappearance of farm life, reminding us that America's modern farms which now "feed the world," are greater by far than they were a hundred years ago. This is quite true but it is the small "personal" farm that has disappeared from the over-all scene, while the big commercial farms have grown. Imagine yourself as the average business man of 1856. There were no automobiles then, so you necessarily had a horse. Perhaps you had two or three. Therefore you had a barn, and pasture, and a hay field. With that much, you probably had a few chickens and some livestock too. Even the smallest house was incomplete without a barn and outbuildings behind it. When the family horse left the scene, farm life for the average person was on its way out. Soon the family car took over the old barn, the pasture was sold for real estate development, and home life lost its rural flavor so much that the American landscape reflected the change.

The modern interpretation of the early American farmhouse has strayed far from the truth. Such ornamentation as imitation split shingles, old-style

16

hardware and decorative shutters will satisfy the average person, but the breathtaking beauty of the original design is usually missing. The secret, it seems, is not in decoration but in the body and outline of old farmhouses. At dusk, when only shapes can be seen, you can best spot the original farmhouses by their silhouettes. The effect of their proportions and lines is vastly different from what is being designed today, yet the differences are often subtle.

A great overhanging roof lends character to a Dutch type house, yet to make it so, might be "too costly." This means that the addition of proper character to the building is not worth that added cost. The few who insist on their house being after the old style, will learn that proper material is no longer available or the price would be too high and it would take too long to build such a house. How strange it is that with our modern time-savers we now have less time; and being the richest nation, we cannot afford homes exactly like those our pioneer farmers built.

Today's "ranch house" often lends itself best to modern air-conditioned living, but except for being Spanish colonial one-floored adobe farmhouses,

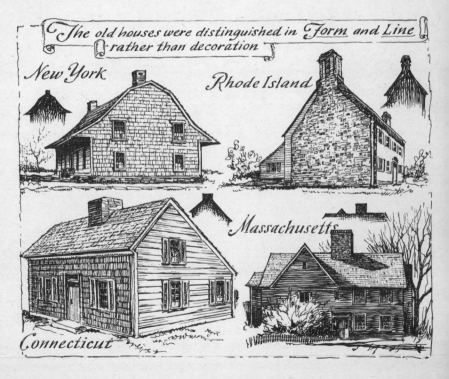

The old houses were distinguished in Form and Line rather than decoration

New York

Rhode Island

Massachusetts

Connecticut

There were Outhouses on the Farms . . . . .

The Outdoor Oven 1820 Pa.

The Blacksmith Shop 1800

Butchering Shed

The Wagon shed

Ohio 1815 Pennsylvania

Spring house 1850

Wash house 1840

Well house

Dove Cote

Virginia 1801

18

The old barn . . .

. . . our first Garage

real ranch houses never were a true architectural style. What we are building might more accurately be called "split-level chicken houses" because the farmer's hen house always had these exact same functional lines.

The arrangement of rooms in the farmhouse was left to the wife, but to the farmer went the task of putting outbuildings in their proper places. The prevailing wind, rain-drainage, the contour of the land and proximity to the farmhouse, decided where the ground cellar, the smoke house, the summer kitchen, the butchering shed, the woodshed, the spring house and the wash house went.

The greatest slant of their roofs always facing the north and their entrances toward the south, outbuildings or "farm-outhousen" were part of a vanished American architecture that has been overlooked. Built with the same architectural care as the home, these buildings were actually as much part of the household, as any room in the farmhouse.

a Classic Privy,
Evergreen plantation, Louisiana
1850

Wall-papered and curtained, discreetly embowered at a considerable distance from the back of the house, was the privy. It was not regarded with the petty humor that surrounds it today, but was taken as seriously as the design of a bathroom is today. The familiar crescent cut into these doors originally designated the building as being one reserved for ladies, for the moon was always regarded as being female. The sun being regarded as male, it was once used as the design on the doors for gentlemen.

.. and Outhouses

Nathan Dean's Privy

EAST TAUNTON Mass.

Pennsylvania Inn 1800

It stretches the modern imagination to think of a privy being architecturally exquisite, yet those built on the southern plantations were delicately designed, often surrounded by statuary, and always in strict keeping with the style of the main house. It is a far cry from the back-house shed that New England country boys overturned as Hallowe'en sport, to the Greek Revival privies of the early south. In many cases where the plantation house was large and rambling, the builder found his fullest expression concentrated in this one small outbuilding, and the privy became a better piece of architecture than the home itself.

There is no evidence that the earliest settlers harvested ice, but they were aware of the low and uniform degrees of underground temperatures. Although most obsolete ground cellars have since caved in or have been covered up, the old farms depended on them for preservation of most food, protecting it against the heat of summer and the freezing of winter. The sketch of the Pennsylvanian ground cellar shows a popular and ingenious arrangement of placing the cellar against the cool walls of the well. Both the well and ground cellar are available to the outside kitchen just above. Some of the old ground cellars are still in use as "root cellars" for storing vegetables, others are supposed to have been used as hiding places for slaves or for protection against the Indians; but vanishing from the farmstead scene, they are really yesterday's kitchen refrigerators.

A few years ago, air-conditioning experts utilized the coolness of cellars to force cooler air up and throughout the house wherever forced hot air is used for heating during the winter. Recently built atomic-bomb shelters have been reported to be the coolest places in the summer; some of them have been used for storage of fruits, being better than refrigerators for that purpose. We now think of a cellar as being the necessary thing to put under a house, but the first farmhouses used them for exactly what the word meant. It comes from the French meaning "pantry" or "store-place for food."

The fact that the earliest farmhouses had dirt floors is a reminder that there was no "foundation-room" or cellar (in the modern sense of the word) beneath. Often the whole farmhouse rested on the ground while the cellar (for food storage) was a short distance away.

If you own an old farmhouse, you might have wondered why your cellar walls have occasional protruding stones. These were put there to support shelves for fruit, and all the jars and crocks of preserves that were kept "cellarwise," at the right temperatures in summer and winter. Only when central heating became part of the house picture, were pantry stores moved upstairs to make room for the furnace and fuel.

The outside cellar door which became so dear to all childhood memories, was originally slanted to take the entrance of garden vegetables in a wheelbar-

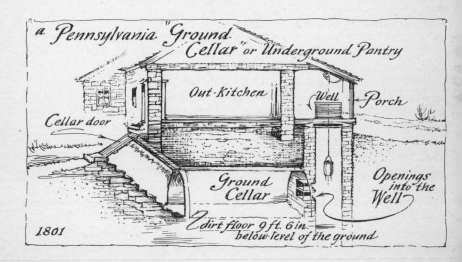

a Pennsylvania "Ground Cellar" or Underground Pantry

Out-Kitchen   Well   Porch

Cellar door

Ground Cellar

Openings into the Well

1801

dirt floor 9 ft. 6 in. below level of the ground

row. It is a pity that modern house design so often forgets a good cellar door, built just for sliding. There are still children who would rather have one than to own their own television.

During the 1800's, farmers learned how to harvest ice and to preserve it in hay. By the late half of the century, the storage and sale of natural ice had become one of the nation's major industries. Railroads were always built to the icehouses which were the biggest single structures of that time. Their vastness can only be imagined by observing the foundations which are still evident along the shores of many northern lakes; some single ice-storage rooms were over five hundred feet long.

The first ice commercially transported was cut from Canal Street in New York City and sent by ship to Charleston, South Carolina, in 1799. From then on it was sent, packed in hay on canal-boats and sailing vessels built just for the purpose, to whichever parts could afford the luxury. In 1805, one hundred and thirty tons of ice were sent by Frederick Tudor on the brig "Favorite" from Boston to the West Indies. There is no record of what the ice weighed at its destination. By 1833, he had begun making shipments of ice to Madras, Bombay, and Calcutta, India.

Ice-making machinery (and finally the electric refrigerator) ended an empire of which there are almost no remaining records. Although they are still being manufactured, ice tongs are already found in antique shops and the old-fashioned wooden iceboxes, scraped down and waxed, are selling well as antique record-player cabinets.

Seventy five years ago, iceboxes were still city equipment. The farmer used his spring house or the well for his refrigerator. The spring house was less hazardous and more accepted for cooling. It was most elaborate wherever the farm kept cows for milk, which of course needed proper cooling. Cows were not as common on the early farm as you might think, for they were kept primarily for meat and for the raising of that famous farm-machine, the ox. Even with a spring house for milk however, there was also a big pail at the well, ready to be lowered with a roast, butter, a can of milk, or whatever needed the cold moistness of underground depths.

It is easy to understand why the old-fashioned shallow well is fast disappearing from the farm scene, being open and dangerous, less sanitary and outmoded by mechanical pumps. Frogs and snakes were regular inhabitants of the water one drank, accepted only because they kept the water clean from the insect world. Yet the water always seemed to taste clearer and better than that from today's house tap. It is interesting to note that the remaining shallow wells go dry much more often than they did a hundred years ago. Many of them have completely exhausted their water supply even without use. This may partly be attributed to milder winters and the less precipitation that this century has had, but mostly it is the result of lands being drained off. Yesterday's forests and swamps and farms gave the land a natural spongelike quality for the storing of water. Today's drained and cleared land accepts rainfall like the wrong side of a blotter. Despite milder weather, floods are now more widespread because water flows over city streets, denuded forests, and "developed" or drained valleys, without soaking deeply into the earth as it used to. The wet decomposed vegetable matter that once composed forest peat and cultivated the virgin timber of yesteryear, has in many places become extinct. The effect upon the landscape is slow and unfortunately unnoticeable within our lifetime.

The brook

If you were to hear that "brooks are disappearing," the idea might seem fantastic. Yet a hundred years ago you could hardly go from here to there without confronting any number of fresh brooks. In the back country you will still find every valley fingered with running streams, but wherever the city has encroached and highways have come within earshot, the earth will have been sufficiently cleared and drained so that there is no rainwater reserve, and the old brooks, you will find, have disappeared.

Yesterday almost any community would have had many swimming holes, but useless mill ponds have been drained and the creeks have dried up. The old swimming hole is indeed a thing of the past for the average youngster.

Mark Twain once said that a farm consists of a creek for swimming, a hayloft for sleeping, outbuildings for exploring and an assortment of haystacks to relax in. You might think that haystacks are the only thing left of the old-time farm scene, but no. Even the smallest farm can now finance the ownership of an automatic baler that packs hay into modernistic boxlike shapes and

23

deposits them across the field with the artistic precision of Picasso. The old hay-wagon that used to wallow down the road with its wheels hidden beneath a mountain of sweet-smelling grass, is now resting out its last years in the sun, behind the barn, and the new-fangled square bales are whisked away in fast trucks, saving much time for something or other. The livestock might not notice the difference, but for the countryman whose youth was filled with the smell and feel of new hay, or the city person who always made a secret wish at the fine sight of a load of hay going past, something cherished has vanished from the farm scene.

The southern plantation is not the sort of thing the average person visualizes when thinking of a farmhouse, yet it also belongs to the historical architecture of rural America. No more valuable examples of buildings have ever been allowed to disappear from a cultural landscape. Symbolic of the many priceless plantations that have vanished from the south, was the famous Uncle Sam Plantation built in 1843. Made of gigantic cypress beams and handmade brick, the main house was the last example of Louisiana Classic. In 1940, the Director of the National Park Service sent a telegram to New Orleans, saying "Have learned of the impending demolition of the Uncle Sam Plantation near Convent, Louisiana. Can demolition be deferred short time pending investigation by National Park Service to determine possibilities for status as a national monument or historic site?" Unfortunately, the telegram arrived after the demolition was almost complete and the waters of the Mississippi had taken back the sand and stones that had once molded an irreplaceable monument of the plantation country.

It is ironic that in many cases, the log-cabin culture of the slave has outlasted the mansion elegance of the old South. The church in the cornfields, the cabin in the woods, and plantation roads worn by farm-wagon wheels and feet of many Negro field workers, have lasted long, and without the help of restoration. Yet there are many-roomed mansions rotting away like symbols of an obsolete past, tombs of the southern landscape.

There are still many log wagon-sheds, log corncribs, and log barns throughout the south, but time has nearly run out on the American log cabin. Built before fences and roads, they were already Americana to the people of the eighteenth century. Their mythological significance was used so much in Presidential campaigns that anyone without a log-cabin background was not considered a homespun American.

The log-cabin culture of the pioneer provided him with his home, his church, and his school. His fences were split logs and his fort was a pointed log barricade. But generally speaking, and contrary to belief, the log-cabin home is more southern than northern. Perhaps because they were built more

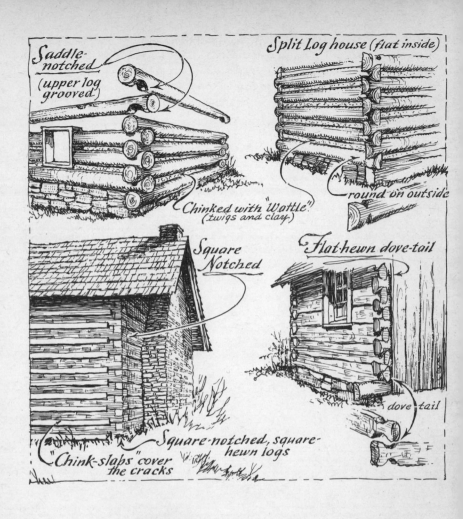

Saddle-notched (upper log grooved.)

Split Log house (flat inside)

round on outside

Chinked with "Wattle" (twigs and clay.)

Square Notched

Flat-hewn dove-tail

dove-tail

"Chink-slabs" cover the cracks

Square-notched, square-hewn logs

Hooded Log cabin Roofs

once covered Mud-and-sticks Chimneys

recently in the south, you will find more examples there, intact against weather and snow rot. There are still nearly ten thousand log buildings left in Georgia, but the decrease from a survey in 1934 when over ten thousand were reported, indicates their complete extinction by the end of this century. Log churches had already disappeared there, and only one log schoolhouse was reported.

The log cabin was introduced to America in Delaware Bay where immigrants from forested Germany and Sweden first settled. In the earliest times there were no log cabins to be found in any of the colonial settlements of the English and Dutch. The New England log cabins of the eighteenth century were of the square-log type, more recent than the round-log cabins of the Swedes in Delaware. Where winter was severe, cabins were dovetail-notched at the joints and "chinked" or filled in at the open spaces with a plaster of clay and twigs called "wattle." A more recent weatherproofing was made by nailing narrow boards over the interstices.

Southern log cabins were generally saddle-notched or made by setting one log astride the other; the upper log was notched to "saddle" the one beneath. There was always a sizable space left between the logs of a southern cabin, which tended to increase as the timber dried and shrunk. "Through the cracks, as you pass along the road," wrote a traveler, "you may see all that is going on within the cabin and at night the light of the fire shines brightly out on all sides."

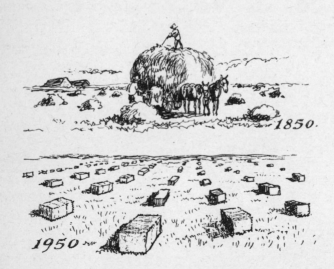

26

FENCES AND WALLS

THE THING that might impress you most about New England is its stone "walls." When they were built, anything forming an enclosure was called a fence. Whether it was made of roots or wood or stone, they were never referred to as walls; they are more properly called stone fences. Furthermore, they were usually topped with one or two rails of wood which have since disappeared into fireplaces as fuel, or rotted away with the years. So fences they really were.

You might wonder why anyone would have gone to such great labor building stone fences through thick forests; they wind over steep wooded mountains and into the deepest glens. But the truth is that when they were built, no forest was there. In fact there were no trees there at all, for the stone fences are no more than neatly piled rocks, gathered during the farm clearings of the eighteenth century. You would hardly think that towering trees could be of second or third growth, grown out of the cleared pasture and cornfields of less than a century ago. But the forest is untiring in its effort to take back its own, and from farmland to woodland is possible in one lifetime. Here is how it happens:

Imagine a farm abandoned as late as 1900. The summer after cultivation ceases, the plowed fields will have become overgrown with weeds. The next year you will find grass and berry seedlings that have blown in with the autumn winds. At the end of five years the fields will be a complete tangle of briars with occasional clumps of birch and juniper from seeds brought in by bird droppings. In ten years these trees will be head high above the briars and in their shade will be hundreds of tiny oak and maple seedlings. In forty years the frail birches will have been crowded out by these stronger trees and with the stone farm fences still winding through them, the fields will look like woodlands that had never seen a plow. Fire or insects and disease may decimate this second-growth forest, or winds may blow it down, but it will miraculously build itself back again into third-growth timber in another fifty years.

The full-page drawing shows typical cleared lands of 1800, when only the marker trees were left standing along with a few farm trees. The result is a pleasant scattering of farmsteads, a main road running parallel with the river. It is interesting to notice that the 1900 highway civilization appears to have been pushed toward the road by the encroaching second-growth forest. Of course the next step could show the late 1900's where the highway civilization will have pushed back the forest again, uncovering the original stone fences of two centuries ago. Today's population will probably double itself in seventy five years, as a second (and the final) forest clearing should have occurred by then.

Our oversea neighbors of two hundred years ago could not believe our fences were anything but rude property divisions or barricades. "A mania for enclosures," they called it, and a typical criticism appeared in a 1780 London paper, saying, "The stripping of forests to build fortifications around personal property is a perfect example of the way those people in the New World live and think."

Our own views of that time appear in a diary of the early 1800's called "Rural Hours." It describes New York State at that time:

"Looking over the country from a height, now that the leaves have fallen, we found the fences attracting our attention. They are chiefly of wood in our neighborhood; zig-zag enclosures of rails, or worm-fences as they are called. We have but few stone fences here; stump fences are often of chestnut, which is considered the best wood for the purpose. Foreigners from the Continent of Europe usually quarrel with our fences, and perhaps they are right; they look upon this custom as a great waste of wood. They say they are ugly in themselves and that an open country, well cultivated, but free from these lines, portrays the idea of a much higher state of civilization, than lands where every half dozen acres are guarded by enclosures. General Lagrange, in the midst of his fine farms of Brie, says that he cannot like our fences. He thinks we should yet learn to do without them; he believes the cost of the wood, and the trouble of putting them up and keeping them in order, might be disposed of to greater advantage in other ways. Hedges, it is feared, will never suit our climate in this State, at least, unless it be our own evergreen shrubs. The

28

1800 ...A solid patchwork quilt of farms... houses scattered everywhere

WALLS and FENCES

MARKER TREES

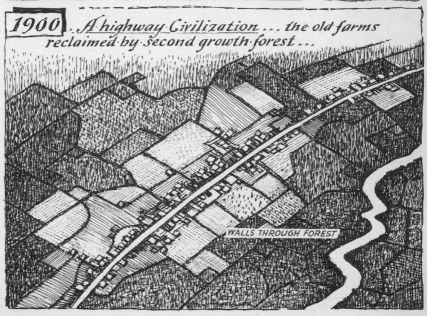

1900 ...A highway Civilization ... the old farms reclaimed by second growth forest...

WALLS THROUGH FOREST

29

FENCE *building was an American Art.*

2 ABOVE, 2 BELOW

New England Cross-and-Rail ...*with stones added*

Vermont

Virginia Stake-and-rail

Straight

Snake

Virginia Snake fence

Bored or Chiselled

POST *and* RAIL

Ohio

hemlock is now coming into use for this purpose, in some neighborhoods. As regards appearances, hedges, close at hand are very pleasing; but at a little distance, they are scarcely an improvement upon the fence: they are still dark, stiff lines, crossing the country with a network of enclosures. Probably we might at least do with much less fencing in this country; it often strikes one that fields are unnecessarily cut up in this way."

What another nation thinks about our fence or whether we have a fence or not might at the moment seem of little importance. But at one time this was a great American issue. Our European critics, we must remember, used fences only for military reasons. Their farms joined into a pattern of landscape with divisions only of hedges or ditches. Their cattle roamed or were watched by shepherds. You have never heard of an early American shepherd because there were too many other things for the pioneer man to do. Fences did the chore just as well, and there were plenty of stones and timber to build them with. The Englishman, with his hedgerows and ditches, chose to regard the American fence in terms of its original derivation from the word "defence." He insisted we were trying to keep people out rather than to keep cattle in.

2,000,000,000
worth of timber
1883

We had our fence problems at home too. In 1883, the Iowa Agricultural Report stated that the United States had six million miles of wood fence at a most conservative cost of three hundred and twenty-five dollars a mile. The dollar in those days was amazingly valuable, so when you realize that this figure amounts to nearly two billion dollars (the same as the national debt for that year) you will begin to realize the importance of the simple fence in the early American picture.

The rail fence not only lavished from four to six rails per section, but was also insatiable in its demand for good wood. As second-growth soft wood lasts only four years or so, the farmer who chose to build for the future used only virgin timber for his fences. A complete acre of first forest growth went into the fences of each ten acres of farmland. A moderate two-hundred-acre farm would thereby require twenty acres of top-grade locust or cedar to enclose it. It has actually been shown in many cases that the western migration of southern farmers was not entirely due to the reported exhaustion of the soil as most history books claim, but also because of an exhaustion of fence material. In this age of wire fencing such a statement seems absurd. But if you depended on rail fence to surround your property at today's cost of sixty dollars a hundred feet, your fifty-acre farm fence would cost close to nine thousand dollars. In 1875 it would have cost about one thousand dollars or more than the worth of the farm.

Not long ago an important job in every American town was that of the fence-viewer. There is nothing for fence-viewers to do today, yet many towns still elect them and pay them for their office. Whether it is done with a Yankee sense of humor or not, the election of fence-viewers in Vermont is still a celebrated custom.

Fence-viewers decided the necessity and the sufficiency of all the fences in their neighborhood. They settled disputes between landowners, and they were liable (by fine) for the neglect of fences within their jurisdiction. Nowadays this strange office is usually bestowed on deserving citizens as a practical joke, but not so long ago, the plug hat and frock coat of the New England fence-viewer was a very official uniform.

The fence-viewer also had his deputies and assistants, two of which carried a Gunter's Chain for measuring acreage and fence mileage. A Gunter's Chain is a linked measuring-device sixty-six feet long, including handles on both ends. It was invented in 1620 by Edmund Gunter, an English mathematician: all road and land measurements since his day were shown on maps in "chains" or divisions of the chain.

To this day, the number sixty-six or denotations of that number occur frequently in historical research or in real estate records. It may be the measurement of a city block (usually three chains to a block, and one to a street), the distance between telegraph poles (one and two chains apart), the width of a canal-way (one chain), or the width of a highway grant (one chain, with the roadbed in the middle). The early "Broad Ways" were of such dimensions as the Duke of Gloucester Street in Williamsburg, Virginia, laid out in 1699 as a "great noble street of six poles" or one and a half chains.

The standard length of a rail or a section of rail fence was eleven feet, so that a fence-viewer could walk along a fence and by apportioning six rails to the chain, he could tell at a glance the size of any field. If he wanted to measure out exact chain-lengths, he could use any eleven foot rail as his measuring-stick.

Shorter distances were measured in rods, also known as "poles" or "perches." Why a rod should be sixteen and a half feet has mystified most students. But sixteen and a half feet happens to be just one fourth of a chain and the rod was once known as a "quarter-chain." Few know why a mile should be 5,280 feet long; but if you multiply a chain by eighty, you will soon find out $(80 \times 66 = 5280)$. Even the mystic 43,560 square feet of an acre is found to be the sum of ten square chains $(66 \times 66 \times 10 = 43,560)$. And it soon becomes obvious that most of our present-day measurements hark back to Gunter and his almost obsolete chain.

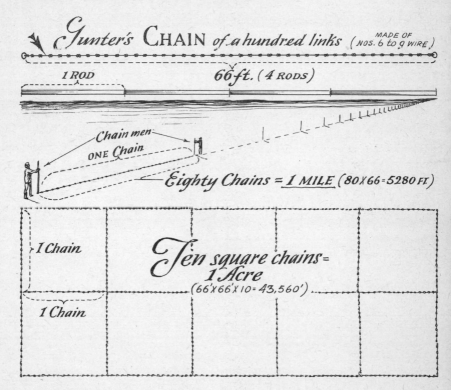

Gunter's CHAIN *of a hundred links* (NOS. 6 to 9 WIRE, MADE OF)

1 ROD

66 ft. (4 RODS)

Chain men
ONE Chain

Eighty Chains = 1 MILE (80×66=5280 FT.)

1 Chain

Ten square chains = 1 Acre
(66'×66'×10= 43,560')

1 Chain

One of the minor mysteries of old fences is the zigzag stone fence. Why would anyone place stones in such a fashion? The answer is simple: the stones were thrown there during a clearing, piled against an existing snake-rail fence. The rails rotted and disappeared, but the stones remained, winding across the land in the same crazy manner. Another small mystery has been old fence-posts that appear to have been charred by fire. Many people presume they survived a grass fire and that the cross-rails which are uncharred, had been

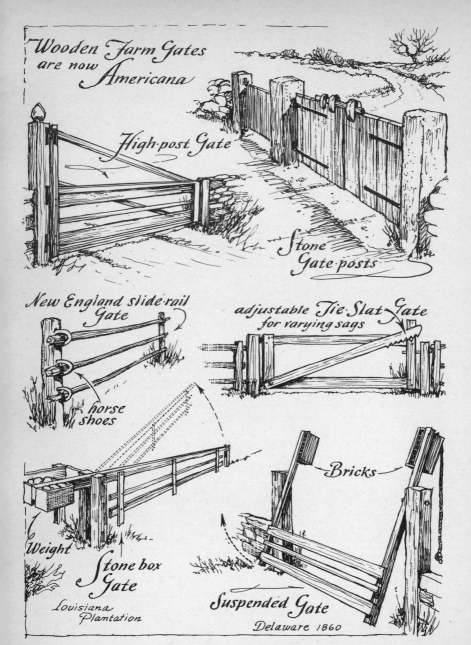

Wooden Farm Gates
are now Americana

High-post Gate

Stone
Gate-posts

New England slide-rail
Gate

horse
shoes

adjustable Tie-Slat-Gate
for varying sags

Weight

Stone box
Gate

Louisiana
Plantation

Bricks

Suspended Gate

Delaware 1860

added later. The truth is that most early fence posts were burned from the bottom and left charred, as a preventative against decay and insect damage. Farmers still use this method, whenever there is no creosote to dip the posts in.

Where the early stone fences came to an opening, there was often a square stone gate-post. The few of these that remain are usually mistaken for monuments or old hitching-posts. Very often the gate and the wall itself have been removed but the stone gate-posts were left because they had been so deeply implanted in the ground. Little has been done about recording early American farm gates: their ingeniousness, if not their historical value, warrants some architectural acknowledgement.

an Ohio fence ax

MILLS

No MATTER where you go in America, you will find millstones. Scattered about the countryside, sunk in the ground as monuments, placed side by side to make walls or for decorating inns and country gardens, people often wonder where so many millstones could have come from, since there are so few old mills to be seen.

The truth is that while most wooden mills have long since disappeared, their indestructible grinding stones have remained behind. "Dressed" with cut grooves, they turned one upon the other, crushing the grain and at the same time pushing it outward to spill off the ends of the stones. Because of a resemblance to plowed farmland, the grooves in millstones were called "furrows" and the plain surface of the stone was called "the land." The interesting patterns that resulted from the different millstone dresses are now almost lost records, yet many a Pennsylvania barn hex sign or farmer's patchwork quilt was inspired by his own preference in millstone design.

The many types of mills and their amazing number were a part of the American picture that is much overlooked today. The smallest village had more water-powered mills than the average person may now see in a lifetime of searching. And all this a mere hundred years ago. Time has run out on the American windmill, but there are still many water-wheeled mills hidden away in the mountain countryside, and people who will travel long distances to buy corn meal from them. Few are aware that they are buying more than quaintness however, for the meal that has absorbed dampness of the millsite, and has been ground under the slow turning of old stones, produces exceptional corn

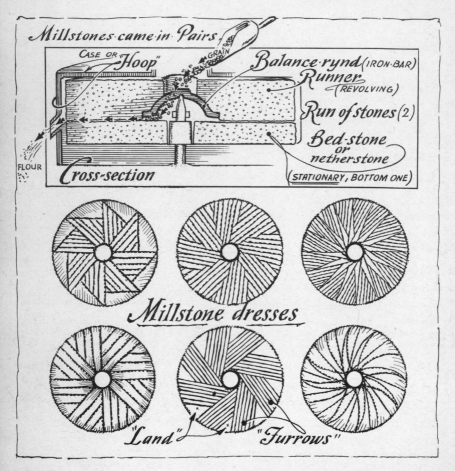

Millstones came in Pairs

CASE OR "Hoop"

GRAIN

Balance rynd (IRON BAR)
Runner (REVOLVING)
Run of stones (2)
Bed stone or netherstone
(STATIONARY, BOTTOM ONE)

FLOUR

Cross-section

Millstone dresses

"Land"   "Furrows"

bread. Yellow Bread, Shortening Bread, Spoon Bread, Hush Puppies, and Corn Meal Dumplings are all-American recipes that were designed for burrstone-ground cornmeal, warm from the mill. "When meal comes to you that way, like the heated underside of a settin' hen," as the old timers put it, "it bakes bread that makes city white bread taste like cardboard."

Because a few restored water-mills are still grinding flour, we might forget that the old time mills did many other jobs. Any chore that could be made lighter by water or wind power became work for the miller. A century ago in a small country community, where you would today find a total of ten shops

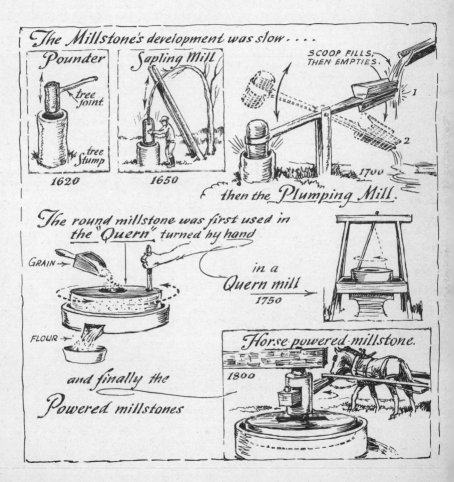

The Millstone's development was slow . . . .

Pounder — tree joint — tree Stump
1620

Sapling Mill
1650

SCOOP FILLS, THEN EMPTIES.
1
2
1700

then the Plumping Mill.

The round millstone was first used in the "Quern" turned by hand

GRAIN →

in a Quern mill
1750

and finally the Powered millstones

FLOUR →

Horse powered millstone.
1800

and a few gasoline stations, you might have found water-powered mill wheels making axes, salt, barrel-staves, hats, pottery, bone-meal, doing calico-printing, and hundreds of other jobs.

The first type of mill in America strangely enough, is still found in the back-mountain country of the south. It is the water-powered pestle which has no wheel or complicated machinery. Used for grinding corn and mashing nuts, these devices called "plumping mills," "beating mills," or "sweep-and-mortar mills," worked by letting a stream of water fill a box on the end of a beam, until the box was so heavy it tipped itself. The stone on the other end of the beam lifted and fell unceasingly into a hollowed stump mortar. It is said that in the still of dawn, the sound of distant plumping-mills drifted across the early countryside and was often mistaken by travelers for Indian drums.

There were few more important cogs in the mechanics of American business than the millers and their mills. Whether there was timber to be cut, salt to be made, flour to be ground or meal to be milled, the village mill was always the link between farmer and industry.

The miller became a price-setter, counselor, buyer, and seller. Often he was banker and always he was the busiest man in town. Among the city fathers he was entitled to be called "master" along with the pastor. His advice on business and banking matters was sought and frequently paid for as would be the services of a lawyer. But mostly, he was host to the entire countryside, an early American politician and the New World's first captain of industry.

His earnings were primarily tolls collected for milling, but the bartering farmer of a hundred years ago seldom used cash. So the miller exacted a portion of the grain that he milled, as payment for his services. The first toll for grinding corn at Plymouth was set at four quarts out of each bushel ground. An act of 1824 in the Statutes of Connecticut allowed the miller to take three quarts of grain for milling each bushel; one quart for each bushel of malt, and only one pint for each bushel of meal. "A miller who took a greater fee," it further stated, "shall pay a fine of two dollars; one dollar going to the owner, the other dollar going to the treasury of the town where the offence was committed."

Because there were few connecting trails and no highways at all, each early village was dependent upon itself for every necessity. Often the smallest community had its own mills for flour, linseed oil, cider, salt, lumber, flax, plaster, tobacco, paint, grain, resin, and so on "down river" to where various smaller mills had set up shop.

In listing subjects of our old-time landscape, you might wonder why mills have been mentioned before roads. The reason for this is that mills were usually built on streams without any regard to land access. The roads came later, beaten as paths to the mills. There are still thousands of "old mill roads," leading only to nearby streams and mill-sites. Many towns and their original roads were built around this arrangement of mills, which explains why most inland towns are located on rivers and streams. The drawing shows the old mills and where each type was located. It explains how the local power of wind or slow-moving water or tide-water or swift streams, designated what type mill should be built there. In the remote backwoods where there was neither sufficient water or wind to operate a mill, animal-power was used.

There is too much controversy over when and where the first American mills were built to make an issue of it here. The first sawmill in Massachusetts is said to have been built in 1633 which was several years before they were introduced in England. In that year the first wind-powered sawmill in Manhattan was erected by the Dutch and the idea spread quickly to Long Island where windmills soon dotted the barren shoreline. Most Long Island windmills pumped sea-water into large shallow evaporating vats for the manufacture of salt. Others made flour and a few sawed wood.

The great seal of New York is built around a windmill design and, though few recognize the fact, the windmill was basic for the beginning of this richest city's industrial career. Very much like the present-day experience of approaching New York's skyline, is an account of nearing Manhattan in 1710: ". . . as we sailed into the harbor the horizon was pierced by scores of windmills, taller than any we have seen elsewhere."

Although we all know what a windmill looks like outside, few are familiar with the inner workings. The drawing shows a "whip" or "spar" with simple sailbars set through it, to be covered with canvas or sailcloth, making the propeller or "sail" that actuated the mill. Notice that the bars close to the hub are set at a steeper angle (20 degrees). This is done because the velocity of the sail increases with the distance from the axle and the sail tips must therefore slice the air at a much greater speed. Sails were usually from thirty to forty feet long which delivered a power of about 65,000 foot-pounds per minute. As wind power was first the problem of the sailor, boat builders became the experts at windmill design. Sailmakers made the canvas vane-covers, and even to the usual captain's hat of the owner, there was a completely nautical air about all windmills.

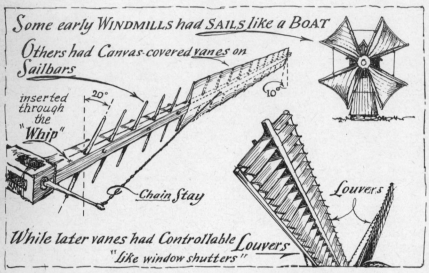

Some early WINDMILLS had SAILS like a BOAT

Others had Canvas-covered vanes on Sailbars

inserted through the "Whip" — 20° — 10°

Chain Stay — *Louvers*

While later vanes had Controllable Louvers "like window shutters"

Because of the necessity for reefing sails during strong winds and the dangers of sudden gusts which sometimes turned mills into monstrous machines of uncontrolled power, a careless miller's life was always a short one. What with being whacked in the head by a spar, thrown aloft from a whirling sail, or being caught in the wheels and ground up in the gears, "killed at his mill" was a frequent miller's epitaph. Millstones used when a fatal accident occurred were henceforth considered unlucky. They were sometimes used as gravestones to mark the last resting place of the unfortunate miller.

One of the advantages that a windmill has over the watermill is that it does not freeze. During the very cold winters of pioneer days, water-wheels were sometimes frozen solidly under tons of ice for the entire winter, while coastal windmills still churned the snow-filled air.

There were some stationary windmills which faced a prevailing ocean breeze, but most windmills had to be turned to face each changing wind direction. There were several devices for turning them into the wind, but most adjustable mills were of the "post" and "smock" type. The post-mill was a mill-house balanced and pivoted on one central post: the whole mill turned (by hand or by horse) until the sails faced properly into the wind. The works of a smock-mill, however, were in a rotating hood raised high above the stationary mill-house below. The smock-mill was later equipped with "flyer-fan" wind-wheels which went into action only when the main sails were aimed wrong; this gadget moved gears which did the mill-turning job automatically. Small smock-mills were of the tower-and-tailpole type, using a long log with a wagon wheel on the end, to turn the tower-head and aim its sails into the wind. Two men could manage this when they were only revolving a

Anatomy of a
SMOCK MILL ·
whose · white · dome · resembles · a Smock

The "Flyer"
only turned if
facing wind ....
then it actuates this gear
and turns Dome back
into the Wind.

Elevator lifts
Grain into
Hopper
which falls
into
Millstones

"smock" or tower-head. But to revolve the big post-mills, where the complete mill-house turned on a pivot, horses or oxen were necessary.

The windmill men were America's first weather experts. A sudden squall, a predicted calm or a shift in the wind might have meant little to a farmer but weather was the wind-miller's stock in trade. When the wind stopped, so did his business; but when the miller got "caught with his sails up" in a squall, the damage could be great. An uncontrolled windmill turning wildly in a storm wind until its sails ripped off must have been an awesome sight.

Sailors in the bay often used windmills as weathercocks and set their sails according to the direction of the mill-sails. Long Island ferries advertised their services as "operating daily, except when the windmills on the opposite shore have taken down their sails."

The builders of the first mills were the millers themselves, but during the nineteenth century, some carpenters and joiners specialized as "millwrights." A typical millwright's advertisement of 1800 read:

> JONATHON ELDREDGE,
> Hartford, Connecticut.
> Builder and joiner of sawmills, barley-mills, snuff-mills, corn-mills, tobacco-mills, mustard-mills, all made to be operated either by water or by horse.

Revolving head. *Stationary tower.* *Tail-pole*

1813 *Mill at Watermill L.I.*

42

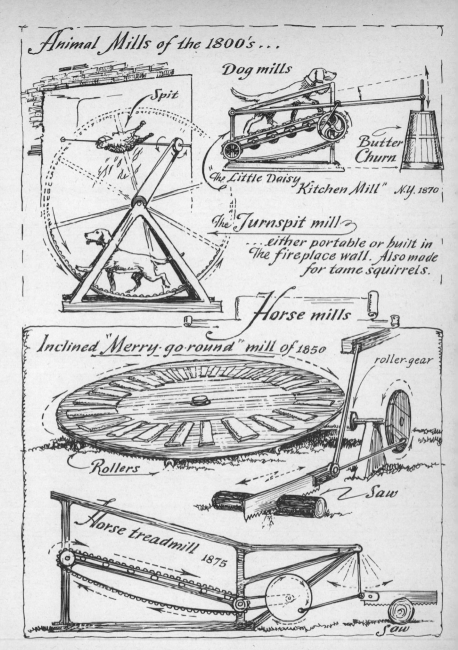

Animal Mills of the 1800's . . .

Dog mills

Spit

Butter Churn

The "Little Daisy Kitchen Mill" N.Y. 1870

The Turnspit mill

. . . either portable or built in the fireplace wall. Also made for tame squirrels.

Horse mills

Inclined "Merry-go-round" mill of 1850

roller-gear

Rollers

Saw

Horse treadmill 1875

Saw

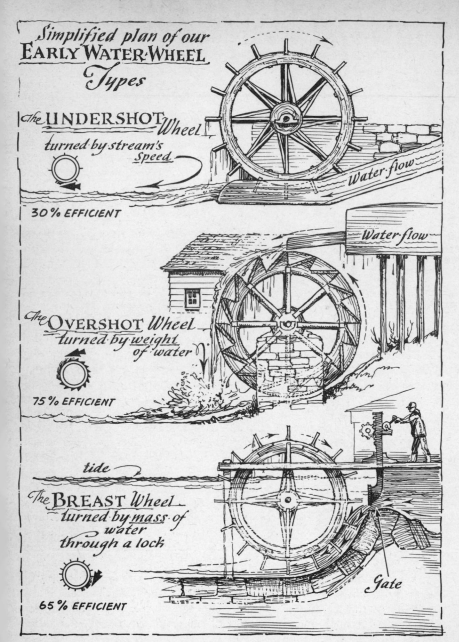

Simplified plan of our
EARLY WATER-WHEEL
Types

The **UNDERSHOT** *Wheel*
turned by stream's
Speed

30% EFFICIENT

Water flow

Water flow

The **OVERSHOT** *Wheel*
turned by weight
of water

75% EFFICIENT

tide

The **BREAST** *Wheel*
turned by mass of
water
through a lock

65% EFFICIENT

Gate

Small horse-power mills were built for private work; they did innumerable jobs around the farm, from sawing wood to threshing grain. The drawing shows popular types as they operated when attached to a wood saw, but horse mills did many other kinds of milling. Although it sounds impractical, such mills designed for small farm animals and dogs were being manufactured and sold less than a hundred years ago. They did much of the necessary milling for farms that were a distance from town. Dogs churned butter, ground snuff, made linseed oil for barn paint and did other light milling. Large farms even employed "turnspit dogs" that ran inside circular treadmills in the kitchen and turned roasting jacks within the fireplace. Records tell of considerable competition as to which dog would take his place in the spit-mill and get his reward in bones when the meat was finally roasted.

The town mill was always a center where people came with their produce, so roads and bridges were soon built to the mills, and towns finally grew up around them. The first reason that the early villages settled near water was because there was no other way for transporting heavy loads. But they ultimately grew and prospered because of their water-powered mills. The Milfords, Milltowns, Millvilles, Millwoods and thousands of American places named after their original water-powered mills, are lasting testimony to the importance of the water-wheeled mill in the early American scene.

The three most popular water-wheel designs, the undershot, overshot, and breast water-wheels were built in a thousand sizes and variations but they were used according to location and the type of waterflow. The undershot wheel was seen mostly in fast-running streams or close to a waterfall, while the overshot wheel was found downstream in slower waterways, usually utilizing a dam, with a raised wooden sluiceway to carry water to the mill, the stream spilled over the top of the overshot water-wheel which was sometimes forty feet high, making it the most powerful type of water-wheel. The breast wheel took its power from its middle or "breast" section. A "high-breast-wheel" received power from above the height of the axle while a "low-breast-wheel" was fed from below axle-height.

The bucket wheel, which was not used for power, was copied from the Far East, where for centuries it had lifted water from river-level and irrigated farmland ten to thirty feet above. Water-wheels have since been used to open canal-locks, to lift canal boats, and to do hundreds of strange jobs of the past. Patents have been taken out to equip canals with automatic water-powered pulling-ropes to eliminate horses. Water-wheels have operated in farmhouses for butter-churning and other household chores, even with an attachment for rocking the baby's cradle and operating spinning wheels and looms.

The metal turbine which is a housed underwater wheel, replaced the wood water-wheel because, operating under the level of winter's ice, it was less

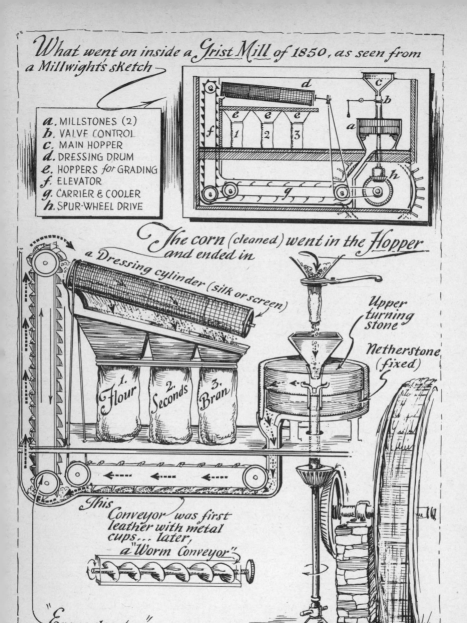

What went on inside a *Grist Mill* of 1850, as seen from a Millwight's sketch

a. MILLSTONES (2)
b. VALVE CONTROL
c. MAIN HOPPER
d. DRESSING DRUM
e. HOPPERS *for* GRADING
f. ELEVATOR
g. CARRIER & COOLER
h. SPUR-WHEEL DRIVE

The corn (cleaned) *went in the Hopper and ended in*

a Dressing cylinder (silk or screen)

1. Flour
2. Seconds
3. Bran

Upper turning stone

Netherstone (fixed)

This Conveyor was first leather with metal cups... later, a "Worm Conveyor"

"*Evans elevator*"

subject to freezing. Many of the early mills are now operating with modern turbines, turning the same ancient machinery, grinding corn and sawing wood as they did before wooden water-wheels began disappearing.

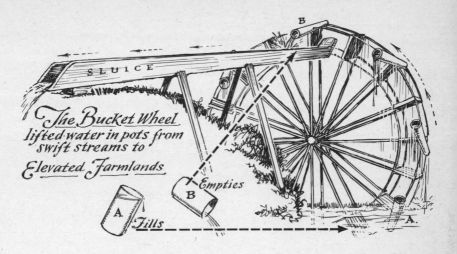

The Bucket Wheel lifted water in pots from swift streams to Elevated Farmlands

Most people accept the water-wheel as a means of turning machinery, but we might wonder what goes on inside the mill. The full-page drawing shows the working of an average grist mill, how the water-wheel turns an upper millstone on top of a lower one, grinding between them the meal which is fed from a middle "hopper." Differently cut millstones made various consistencies of flour, or they ground different kinds of products. Farmers often waited for the mill to change to certain favorite millstone dresses and millers had special days for milling produce in season. The mill-wheel sometimes took the place of a giant arm, turning a pestle in a mortar for grinding snuff or extracting oils from crushed seeds. The snuff-mill shown in the drawing is located below a room in North Kingston, Rhode Island, in a house where Gilbert Stuart was born. This was the type of equipment many farmhouses employed, almost as we might use a mix-master in our kitchen.

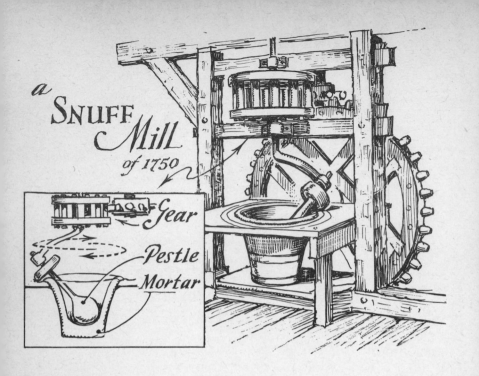

a SNUFF Mill of 1750

Gear

Pestle

Mortar

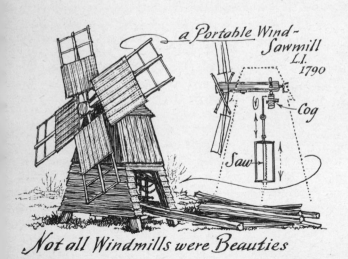

a Portable Wind-Sawmill L.I. 1790

Cog

Saw

Not all Windmills were Beauties

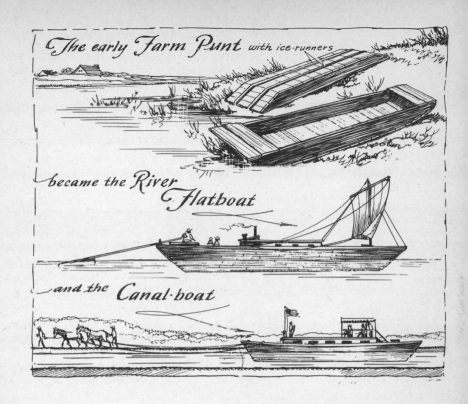

The early Farm Punt with ice-runners

became the River Flatboat

and the Canal-boat

THE SLUICEWAY that led water from the millpond to the mill was usually a boxlike wooden canal. Often it stretched over a thousand feet; when it was longer, a channel was dug in the ground and the American canal was born. For the idea set inventive minds to work, and by 1750 farmers had tried their hand at irrigation canals; canals were dug for floating logs across-country; where the sluiceway was big enough to hold a small flatboat, heavy loads of grain could be floated to the mill. Perhaps the idea grew from watching children sail toy boats along the sluiceway stream, but the biggest promise for transportation in America was the canal. Wherever there was water, a roadway of water could be built.

Few farms were without one or two punts on their ponds. They were used as sleds in the winter and as boats during summer. When the ice in the pond was dangerously thin, the punt with its ice-runners underneath was the ideal vehicle for hauling anything from stones to wood and farm produce. They are best remembered as boats for eeling and fishing, without much thought to design and put together hastily by any handy farmer. Yet the pattern developed into the famous river flatboat, the industrial canal-boat and the present-day barge.

By 1800, roads had begun to web their way through the American wilderness. But although they were well represented on maps of the countryside, they were actually not as pronounced as were some of the buffalo and deer paths. Their use was entirely dependent upon the weather. When rain fell, the rough fields or even the forest was more passable than the ribbons of mud that were our first roads. Such passageways were confined to emergency trips or wherever water travel was impossible. From the beginning, Americans accepted waterways as the best method of traveling, or for moving goods from one place to another.

The Ohio and its tributaries offered a smooth highway of over a thousand miles. The Mississippi and Missouri waterways spread from New Orleans upward and out toward the Great Plains. If there were goods to be moved wherever the rivers flowed, roadways were never even considered. In Philadelphia, coal cost less when shipped from Newcastle, England than it did when hauled over the road from nearby Richmond, Virginia. The scale of prices in 1800 showed that one ton of merchandise transported from overseas cost about the same as it would if hauled over the roads in America for thirty

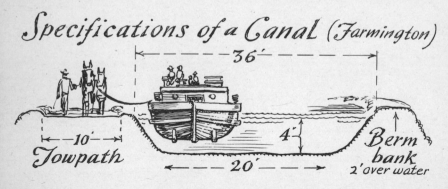

Specifications of a Canal (Farmington)

36'

10'
Towpath

20'

4'

Berm bank
2' over water

miles. This, plus the uncertainty of weather, made the sloop and flatboat the freight-car and motor truck of yesterday. The cross-country "road map" was more often a map of the rivers and streams with trails to portage from one waterway to another.

It took a month and a half to drift by flatboat from Pittsburgh to New Orleans and during the early 1800's about twenty thousand craft went downstream. The trip with the current was a one-way affair, so when one's final destination was reached, the boat was usually broken up and the timbers were used as house lumber. Many of the southern homes were built of ship's timber that came from a thousand miles away, which often explains northern-grown woods in their panels and staircases.

River flatboat design became more and more advanced and the idea of smooth water-travel proved to be sure, economical, and safe. A network of canals such as had already solved the transportation problem overseas, seemed to be necessary for the growth of the country. Every man with an engineering background—and some with no more than a political yearning—made his own inventive contribution to the world of canal design. Southern planters dug ditches and floated their tobacco to the river wharf instead of hauling it by horse. The whole country had become canal-minded.

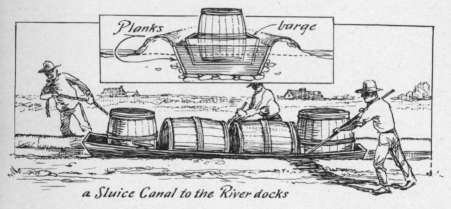

a Sluice Canal to the River docks

A first canal was built around the falls of the Connecticut River at South Hadley Falls, Massachusetts, in 1793. There were no locks, but boats were sailed into movable caissons and hauled to higher levels by water-powered cable-pulls. The first through-way canal was the Santee Canal in South Carolina, started in 1794 and finished in 1800. The first great canal was Clinton's "Big Ditch," the Erie Canal, and hundreds of connecting canals were immediately proposed. The wonder of it all was that there were no American engineers at the time, and neither was there any excavating machinery. With no more than the ingenuity of local surveyors and such simple tools as shovels and wheelbarrows, these man-made rivers were cut through the most difficult countryside. Using only timbers cut from the forest by hand and oxen to haul

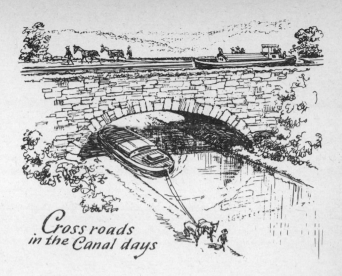

Cross roads in the Canal days

stones, canals were bridged and made to cross one over the other, into a lace-work of inland waterways.

Today you will find modern railroads using ancient canal-beds for their own trackbed. Sometimes you will motor through a high-walled section of farm-land that was first a canal-way before it became the highway. You might have thought that ditch running parallel to a railroad was for drainage. Actually it was once a canal; the present railway tracks are built on what was once the towpath. Or you might come upon some lofty bridge piers across a river where there is no roadway: you would hardly suspect that they once held a wooden aqueduct and canal-way, carrying it and the canal traffic high across the roaring river below.

Even to touch upon the rich story of American canals would necessitate a complete book. But to give a good example of their flourishing life and quick disappearance from our landscape, let us look at the Farmington Canal of New England, which was over eighty miles long. It opened three years after the completion of the Erie Canal (1828) and it operated until a little over a hundred years ago. Today few people know of this big ditch, dug by hand through the rocky New England hills, with locks that lifted boats as high as three hundred and ten feet. Few New Englanders have even heard of it.

Until the Farmington Canal failed because of the coming of railroad trans-portation and various difficulties with unfriendly landowners, its career was filled with a wealth of romance and historical interest. Much of its right-of-way was obtained through condemnation without proper payment, so angry

The Farmington Canal through Connecticut, typical
of America's many Vanished and Forgotten Waterways.

Now just a deep Lane
through Milldale

Great Salmon arch
at Granby

Part of the 7-piered Aqueduct
over the Farmington River
(these 3 piers remained)

remains of
Canal with
Railroad on the
towpath.
(One mile south of
Cheshire, Conn.)
1920

Canal Passage through New
Haven, used as a railroad bed

landowners either blocked off tributary streams used as the canal's water supply or dug away the embankments and let the water out.

Some farmers complained that their farms were cut in two. The canal company was forced to build suitable bridges across, but there was always a hay-wagon tipped into the canal, a bridge burned, or other trouble to contend with. Some farmers sued because the canal had taken away their water supply and others because the canal leaked onto their lands and flooded the crops. One farmer settled his grudge against a neighbor by breaking the canal embankment and flooding his enemy's farm; of course, the damage to the canal was much more than that to the flooded farm. The canal's lifetime was marked by floods, by ice during the winters and by a drought in 1843 which closed the canal for the entire summer. But the venture was far from being an entire loss. There were splendidly equipped packet-boats carrying passengers and freight from New Haven to Northampton in two days.

There were several stops along the way to change horses and for meals: people went to church by canal, shopped in nearby villages and enjoyed dancing and entertainment on the way. At Farmington there was a three-story brick hotel (later part of the Porter School) built to accommodate canal travelers. There are now communities in Connecticut that rose from back-country farmland because of the inland waterway, yet the present-day inhabitants could never believe that their village was the result of a canal that carried ships past its inland mountainsides.

On the Fourth of July in 1825, when Governor Oliver Wolcott turned the first spade of earth to commemorate the beginning of the Farmington Canal, his spade broke. It was said to be an evil omen and that the company would not last. However, it was the only part of a great network of canals proposed to supply New England that was ever finished. Although the project was dug with no more than spades, and by the sweat of farmers and common laborers, an airplane pilot could now trace its path across the entire State of Connecticut. Towns have sprung up along its web, railroads and highways have adopted its bed, and the countryside of New England is richer for its having been.

In 1848 the Farmington Canal boats docked for the last time. The taverns along the way became dwelling houses. At New Haven the canal's end became the site of a railway roundhouse. Farmers dammed up portions of the canal for their own duck-ponds. Farm boys found the lowering water filled with pickerel and cattails and the joys of a swimming hole. The Farmington, like thousands of other canals in America, was disappearing back into the landscape.

Significant of what canals meant to American business is an account of the opening of the Erie Canal from the New York State Historical Collection of 1841.

"The celebration procession," it reads, "moved in the following order:

"The Journeymen Tailors. The Butchers with Butcherboys, mounted and wearing aprons. The Tanners and Tannerboys in floats with men at work. The Skinners. The Cordivainers with six men at work making shoes. The Hatter's Society had a car with eight men at the kettle and others in different operations of hat-making. The Bakers with white hats. The Journeymen Masons. The Coopers in a car with men making barrels. The Chairmakers. The Potters and then the Saddlers. The Shipwrights had a model of a line battleship on wheels, drawn by ten horses. The Comb-makers, the Printers, the Bookbinders and Tinplate Workers came next, followed by the Societies and Associations of New York Industries. Many of these people will, through the canal, ply their business in distant places and stimulate trade that the horse and wagon might never reach."

What the canal meant to peddlers involves many an amusing tale. There were Yankee Peddlers who seldom left the canals, living at the inns along the way, buying and selling household equipment heavier than their wagons could have carried. Some of the first pianos were carried across country by canal, played as they went and ending wherever a purchaser was found. People often met the weekly boat from the big town which usually had one or two actor-peddlers aboard. In costume, perched atop the barge, singing and playing a flute or a banjo, his performance was ended by a brisk sale of Kickapoo Remedy or tin-plate kitchenware. The sale was always worth a repeat performance at the inn if the boat captain was agreeable, then on to the next town.

The Circus comes to town by Canal Boat

Circuses sometimes traveled by canal. Their entrance into town with a band playing on the upper deck and acrobats cavorting from the towpath to the canal-boat, like as not, with one of the elephants pulling the craft, was a sight to delight our great grandparents.

For a fee, handbills were handed out by the captain, and advertisements were displayed on the sides of the boat. Anything from a banner to a ten-foot billboard proclaimed the merits of Dr. Girard's Ginger Beer, Indian Worm-cure or the arrival of a minstrel show.

Excursions were advertised, particularly on holidays. For fifty cents you could have a round-trip day of it, with music and entertainment. Many of the boats specialized in carrying ice from the mountain lakes. The Morris Canal in New Jersey offered "cool summer rides, accompanied by a shipment of ice", just the way to relax while going to town. Long after the Morris Canal closed, New York canoe clubs used the route to paddle to Lake Hopatcong. Dozens of canoes might reach the end of the line at one time, filled with canoeists bronzed by the sun of fifty miles along the canal.

ROADS

EVEN TODAY, when you send anything across country you refer to it as "shipping." Express companies still have "shipping charges" and "shipments" arrive whether they come by freight car or by motor van. This stems from the time not long ago when freight sent across-country went only by ship or canal boat. Dirt roads were just not designed for freight and even the six-foot-high wheels of a prairie schooner bogged in rain or snow, when laden down.

The canals had taken even some of the tourist business, for the comfort of living-room steadiness and the pleasure of seeing the countryside float gently by without the discomfort of corduroy log-roads and jouncing "thank-you-ma'ams," made up for slowness. Charles Dickens remarked that no person should ever go by road in America who couldn't get there by boat. In describing a coach trip on our roads he wrote, "A great portion of the way was over what is called a corduroy road which is made by throwing trunks of trees into a marsh, and leaving them to settle there. The very slightest of the jolts with which the ponderous carriage fell from log to log, was enough, it seemed, to have dislocated all the bones in the human body. . . . Never, never once that day, was the coach in any position, attitude or kind of motion to which we are accustomed!"

Even as late as 1870 many roads in New England were only clearings through forest, with few level stretches and often with stumps left in the middle of the road. In that year the Governor of Connecticut wrote, "What we complain of under the present condition of affairs is that all four wheels of our wagons are often running on different grades. This kind of road will throw a child out of its mother's arms. We let our road-makers shake us enough to the mile to furnish assault and battery cases for a thousand police cases."

Despite the hardships of coach travel, many remarkable stagecoach trips were accomplished which seem impossible today. For example, a trip from New York City to Philadelphia in this age can take up the good part of our day: even by airplane, which necessitates about an hour's road traffic to and from the airports at both ends, it is regarded as a good journey. Yet read an account of the same trip at the beginning of the century:

"Mr. Hyde's coach left the Holland House in New York at 5:55 A.M. and drew up at the Belvedere Hotel in Philadelphia at 3:20 P.M. The return trip was undertaken six minutes later and ended in front of the Holland House once more at 3:36 A.M. the next morning. The round trip of nineteen hours and thirty five minutes required seventy eight horses which were distributed along the route. Only one driver was needed however, and he was as fresh as a daisy when he stepped from the box." The coach was without shock-absorbers and its compartment was only thinly cushioned, with two thirty-six-inch seats facing each other. One movable seat contained a chamber pot, which must have added to the many rattles.

The use of seventy-eight horses might astound those who are not aware of how stagecoaches operated and that they were vehicles designed to pick up fresh horses at different "stages" along the way. But even with fresh horses, the average stagecoach journey was sometimes such an ordeal that riders made out their will before starting.

as Protection against Wash-outs
and Resting-places for Oxen
and horses on their way uphill,

(rain drains)

"Thank-you-ma'ums"
were _not_ poor road design.

The ride from New York to Boston first took six days and each lap covered eighteen hours of road travel. The day started at two or three o'clock in the morning, when the traveler (who usually slept in his clothes) was routed from his lodging at the stagecoach inn for the next lap. The New York-Boston trip, however, was first planned as a pleasure ride and made to appear attractive in its first advertisement in the New York *Journal* for June 25, 1772:

THE STAGE COACH
between
NEW YORK AND BOSTON

Which for the first time sets out this day from Mr. Fowler's Tavern (formerly kept by Mr. Stout) at Fresh Water in New York will continue to go the course between Boston and New York, so as to be at each of those places once a fortnight coming in on Saturday evening and setting out to return by way of Hartford on Monday morning. The price to passengers will be 4d. New York, or 3d. lawful Money per Mile and Baggage at a reasonable price. Gentlemen and Ladies who choose to encourage this useful new and expensive Undertaking, may depend upon good Usage, and that the Coach will always put up at Houses on the Road where the best Entertainment is provided. If on Trial, the Subscribers find Encouragement they will perform the Stage once a week, only altering the Day of setting out from New York and Boston to Thursday instead of Monday Morning.

The Post Riders who carried the mail along the Boston Post Road ran on a twice-a-week schedule. Two men started out at the same time, one from New York City and the other from Boston. Speeding toward each other, they met half-way in Connecticut to exchange saddlebags and then set out in opposite directions. This half-way switch was accepted as a clever time-saver until it was realized that both riders traveled the same distance and no time was actually saved at all. The only convenience was that the riders were able to sleep in their own beds more often. At least the important two-hundred-and-fifty-mile link between Boston and New York had a day-and-night mail service, and by 1765 Benjamin Franklin boasted that a letter mailed in Philadelphia was sure to reach Boston by three weeks.

The early post office was first responsible for the erection of milestones, because postal rates were set rigidly, according to mileage. Benjamin Franklin devoted a great deal of his time as Postmaster General to the placing of milestones, and many of the stones standing in Pennsylvania and New England are said to have been set in place by Franklin himself. A more logical story is that he made special trips to inspect them, after they had been placed. He did make such a New England journey by chaise while his daughter accompanied him most of the way on horseback.

Some of the earliest milestones were set on the road between Philadelphia and Trenton. They were paid for in fines by the Philadelphia Contributionship for the Insurance of Houses from Loss by Fire. Thomas Wharton and Jacob Lewis were contracted to make and place these stones, "the distance of a mile, one from the other, with the number of miles from Philadelphia to be cut solidly in each stone." Starting from Front and Market Streets on May 15, 1764, the Surveyor General of the Province set them all in place, possibly the first American milestones. He used a "clacker" set on the wheel of a wagon that measured out each mile, but the New England milestones were set by surveyors who laid out eighty Gunter's chains to the mile "because no two wheels turned the same number of times on a Yankee road."

Putting in the Milestones...
a "clacker" counted the revolutions
of a wheel for one mile

CIRCUMFERENCE
MULTIPLIED·BY
REVOLUTIONS = MILEAGE

Before 1800, postal rates were often scaled to individual miles but the nineteenth century saw rates regulated and scaled to five- and ten-mile proportions. The *Farmer's Almanac* of 1813, for example, gives rates "of every single letter by land" as follows: "Every letter composed of a single sheet of paper not conveyed above thirty miles six cents. From thirty to eighty miles, ten cents. From eighty to one hundred and fifty miles, twelve and a half cents. From one hundred and fifty to four hundred miles, eighteen and three fourth cents. Over four hundred miles, twenty five cents." For each extra sheet of paper used, you were charged an additional postal rate. This is a reason why the early magazines and newspapers were printed on one sheet and folded over.

Envelopes were unknown before the early part of the 1800's and not until 1847 did stamps become necessary. *Historic Oyster Bay* tells of some children who went to postmaster James Caldwell's house to post a letter. "Mr. Caldwell did not take their money in the usual manner on this day, but handed them back a tiny picture of Benjamin Franklin which they were told to glue to the corner of the letter. It was the first postage stamp, of which there were two kinds, five and ten cents with portraits of Franklin and Washington." Because of a shortage of five-cent stamps, you were allowed to cut Washington (a ten cent stamp) in half and use it that way.

17 Miles to Litchfield. A Connecticut marker from about 1763

19 Miles from Philadelphia Placed on May 15, 1761

At first, letters were entrusted to the stage driver or even to friends traveling in the right direction. Deliveries were something special, usually left in a pigeonhole of the nearest tavern desk, but sometimes left by the stage driver in some secret crevice of a tree. When a farm was located far from town, the farmer was often clever enough to place a watering trough for stagecoach horses on the road, with a mailbox nearby. This afforded a pardonable stop for the coach, and time enough for the driver to put mail in the box.

The FIRST American Mail box →

Boots were made entirely by hand in those days, often fashioned by the wearer himself; therefore there was something especially personal about each man's boot. So it was the custom to put one's boot out for the collection of any personal message, and some of the first "mailboxes" of rural delivery were no more than farm boots nailed to a post.

The "deerpath" roads of yesterday shock most of us in this age of wide highways, yet the real wonder was that without road-building equipment, roads were possible at all. It is almost beyond conception that roads a thousand miles long, and canals through mountainous countryside, could be dug with no more than shovels and wheelbarrows. Without blasting or dredges, roads, slight as they were, went through the wilderness in a surprisingly quick manner.

On May 10, 1776, the Congress voted a military road to be built between Newburg, Vermont, and the Province of Canada. This road had already been recommended by General Washington to facilitate the march and return of troops in that area. In forty-five days, a group of one hundred and ten men working for the pay of ten dollars a month, pushed fourteen miles through hardwood forests and steep mountainsides, to make a road suitable for wagons. That is close to two thousand feet a day, including bridge-ways and logways over soft ground, cutting down virgin trees, removing the stumps and piling rocks to the side of the road. Food and a half a pint of rum were thrown into the thirty-cents-a-day wage, and the road which was built at almost the speed of a slow walk was considered no great feat in those days, even though the peril of Indian attack was included.

This road was continued in 1779 by Colonel Moses Hazen (whose name has ever since been attached to it) with a labor force of local militia. The Hazen Road is a military road in design, because it follows hilltops, avoiding valleys and swampy places. The later mill and factory roads which were guided by economic motives, followed the rivers and valley streams where industries settled. Military roads, often a rod wide, crossed water at right angles and sought the protection of ridges and high ground. Both the picturesque road that hugs the river bank, and the rod-wide lane are destined to disappear from the American landscape.

What we now refer to as a country lane was once the minimum width for American private right-of-way roads. The lane land-grant was one rod wide, with an eight-foot roadbed. The same law stated that "private roads shall not be more than three rods wide." Few of the early rod-wide lanes remain with their rows of stone fences or tall trees only sixteen and a half feet apart. The foliage that converged overhead to form a tunnel of green was an unforgettable pleasure: the disappearance of such pathways makes the simple pastime of "swinging down a shady lane" a vanished American delight.

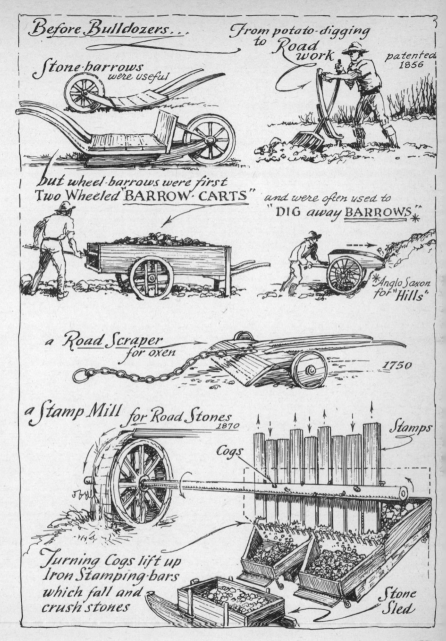

Before Bulldozers...

Stone·barrows were useful

From potato·digging to Road work

patented 1856

but wheel·barrows were first
Two Wheeled "BARROW·CARTS" and were often used to "DIG away BARROWS"

*Anglo Saxon for "Hills"

a Road Scraper for oxen

1750

a Stamp Mill for Road Stones
1870

Stamps

Cogs

Turning Cogs lift up Iron Stamping·bars which fall and crush stones

Stone Sled

Lane-width

←------ *16 ½'* ------→

There was once a popular theory that a gently undulating road is less fatiguing to horses than a level one. "The alternations of ascent, descent, and levels call into play different muscles, allowing some to rest while others are exerted, and thus relieving each in turn." This theory was used in New York's subway and elevated railroads but applied to machinery instead of animal muscles. A gentle dip between each station got the train under way quicker, while the upgrade of the next station, worked with the brakes to bring the train to a stop.

It seems strange that in times when our roads were no more than rivers of mud, people should worry about undulating roads or the picturesqueness of their curvatures. Yet those were romantic times when men were both farmers and designers, poets were statesmen and artists were engineers. One of the most controversial details about road design was whether roads should be straight or curved. Coleridge who considered himself a road expert, said,

> The road the human being travels,
> That on which blessing comes and goes, doth follow
> The river's course, the valley's playful windings,
> Curves round the cornfields and the hill of vines.

"Straight roads over an uneven and hilly country may at first view, when merely seen on the map, be pronounced a bad road," said De Witt Clinton, "for the straightness must have been obtained by submitting to steep slopes in ascending the hills and descending the valleys." "Straightnesss should always be sacrificed to obtain a level, or to make a road less steep," said road expert Dr. Gillespie in 1873, and many others joined the unbelievable fight against straight roads. This, of course, did not pertain to city streets, but it did pertain, for the sake of beauty, to pleasure drives. Some of the best road designers were known for their use of Hogarth's "line of grace," and their ability to put a road through a park or cemetery that deceived the traveler into believing he was traveling over a large area and "lulled him into a relaxation of curves." The Greenwood Cemetery Road shown in the plan from an early road-builder's manual and considered a gem, illustrates this principle. It would be a road-builder's nightmare today.

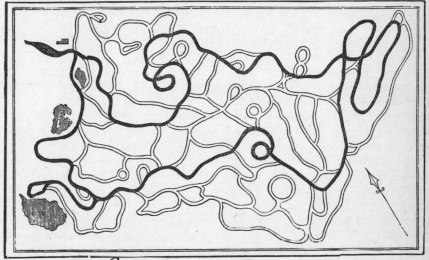

Greenwood Cemetery

There are still crushed-oyster-shell roads along the seacoast, left over from the time before the development of plank roads, These shell roads are the only ones remaining from that period of experimentation with everything from crushed coal to corncobs. One material that promised to stay longer

65

(Figure panels: 1. pile timber in road — 9' — Road — 5'; 2. fire it under hay and (Hay) — Prepare ditches Ⓐ and Ⓑ; 3. Cover with earth from ditch so wood smolders and Chars; 4. Put earth back; Rake coals into a Roadbed — 2' high — 1' high — 15' Road)

than it actually did was charcoal. A road-building manual of 1869 explains how a charcoal road was built. "Timber from six to eighteen inches thick through, and cut twenty five feet long, is stacked lengthwise in the middle of the road and covered with straw. By firing this, and at the same time covering it with earth from the sides of the road, the timber becomes charcoal. When properly charred, the earth is removed to the side of the ditches: the coal is raked down to a width of fifteen feet, leaving it two feet high at the center and one foot high in the middle. The road is then complete."

The manual did not mention the forests that were being laid waste to produce these charcoal roads, but few people considered that anyway. The truth is that more of America's forest wealth went into charcoal, either for smelting iron or for making roads, than ever went into building lumber or for heating purposes. Timber was only worth what it cost to cut it. The manual adds that "a charcoal road in Michigan cost six hundred dollars a mile; two are being built in Wisconsin at about five hundred dollars a mile. It is probable that charcoal will fully compensate for the deficiency of limestone and gravel in western sections where roads are constructed through forests. Charcoal costs a fourth of the expense of limestone."

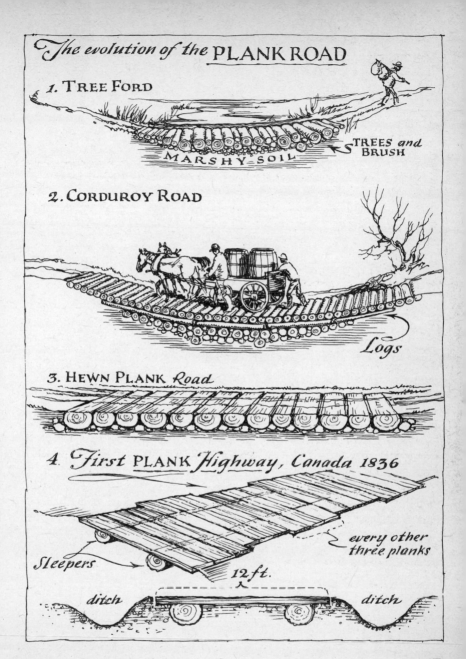

The evolution of the PLANK ROAD

1. TREE FORD

TREES and BRUSH

MARSHY SOIL

2. CORDUROY ROAD

Logs

3. HEWN PLANK Road

4. First PLANK Highway, Canada 1836

Sleepers

every other three planks

12 ft.

ditch   ditch

WOODEN ROADS

THE ONLY REMINDER of the American plank road might be those highways which still bear the name. The fifteen-mile Paterson Plank Road in New Jersey which was once known as the Farmer's Railroad to New York, is now buried under the modern roadways, yet old residents still refer to the route as the plank road. Only seventy-five years ago, the whole country was webbed with such paths of wood, enough to level forests of pine and hemlock, tamarack, oak, and walnut. In 1875 there were close to three thousand miles of plank roads in New York alone, and by 1880 the idea had spread to every other state.

The first plank road was possibly those short inclined wooden entrances that led to covered bridges, but the first registered plank highway on this continent was the one built in Canada in 1836. This road had twenty-inch planks lying lengthwise, but the next Canadian plank road had "skewed" planks, set diagonally at a forty-five degree angle. When the idea struck the United States, however, the custom was to lay planks directly across the road, at right angles to the direction of the highway.

The word "highway" came from old Europe, where there was always a smooth private road for the King, with an adjoining lower shelf road for commoners. The American plank roads which so resembled that arrangement, with their elevated plank sections and adjoining dirt "turn-off" roads, were at once called Highways and the name has stuck.

Canadian plank roads introduced the idea of using irregular edges, so that wagons could "climb" back onto the planks after having gone off to the dirt turn-off to pass another wagon. A smooth edge would have caused the wagon wheels to just slide along the straight-edge without mounting the planks. At first, every other three planks were set a-jog about four or five inches, but this spacing caused very small wheels to get hung and stuck in the opening. The American plank road at once adopted the idea of projecting every other plank four inches from the edge. This not only enabled wheels to climb back aboard again, but caused an effective series of short warning bumps when the wagon got too close to the edge. Likewise, wherever a sharp curve was approached, planks were set a small distance apart to produce a rumble and awaken the sleepy driver to alertness.

Plank-road design varied, but the design of New York State roads became an average plank-road dimension that was copied throughout the

68

country. The usual road grant was of one chain width (66 feet), with a roadbed of thirty feet and a plank path at least eight feet wide. With ditches for drainage, an earth turn-off track of about twelve feet, the finished plank road was covered with sand or wood shavings. Even today, a well-kept plank road would make a more desirable highway for horse-and-wagon traffic than a modern concrete highway. Horses when given a free rein, on a dirt turn-off, would automatically pull up onto the plank road where the going was perfect both for wagon wheels and horse's hoofs.

The planks themselves were from three to four inches thick and from nine to sixteen inches wide. They were laid on top of "sleepers" or rails. Canadian plank roads put two spikes in each plank, nailing it to the sleeper, but the American custom was more often to lay planks loose and let gravel and their own weight keep them in place. Even when the planks went across a bridge, they were laid loose, and up until a few years ago, the thunder of planks when a car drove across a small bridge, was pleasant relaxation to any cross-country driver.

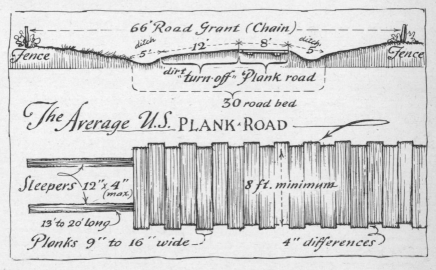

Sleepers varied in size from four by six inches to four by twelve (laid flat) but many small roads left them out altogether. Long stone rollers were used to flatten out the road and push sleepers into the dirt before laying the planks on top. Hidden away in many a barn are still those stone rollers which often baffle the antiquarians.

The cost of a plank road, including gate-houses and surveying, averaged a thousand dollars to two thousand dollars a mile. An oak road was built to last for twelve years and a pine road was considered good for four. The New York Senate reported in 1870 that "plank roads are a more profitable investment than gravel or stone: they never break up in winter thaws or fall away in spring freshets the way paved roads do." Canada reported costs to be four to one in favor of wood.

As plank roads were originally built for profit by tolls, it might interest the student to learn exactly what such tolls were. The New York Plank Road Law established the following tolls in the 1870's:

"Any vehicle drawn by one horse, ¾ cents per mile. For vehicles drawn by two horses, 1½ cents per mile, and ½ cent additional for each extra horse. For a horse and rider, or a led horse, ½ cent. For every score of sheep, swine or neat cattle, one cent per mile."

Plank roads ended where the towns began, but the efficiency of wood paving still carried on its crusade. Every retired man with a flare for engineering and an eye toward an easy income, designed his own kind of wooden brick or patented paving. Most popular was a wooden block pavement set between thin wooden planks and covered with gravel or tar.

"Wood is better than stone for pavement," wrote Frank Johnson, M.D., in a pamphlet for "Nicolson Pavement," in 1867, "for any pavement that increases the destruction of shoe, horse, vehicle, chaise, or decreases comfort and convenience is not economical though it costs nothing and lasts forever."

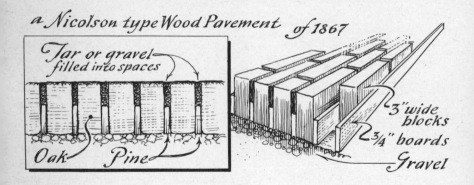

a Nicolson type Wood Pavement of 1867

Tar or gravel filled into spaces

Oak   Pine

3" wide blocks
¾" boards
Gravel

THERE ARE THOSE who have the ability to recognize unchanged scenes, who can easily step into the picture of today and listen to the past. To those favored few, covered bridges are always irresistible. Like old watermills, they seem to echo clearer the mood and sounds of the past where in the shadowed recesses of a stream and along the banks of winding dirt roads, American life first developed.

At one time covered bridges were as much a part of any journey as are today's traffic signals. Most country roads followed the banks of a river and at every bend there was one or more of these barnlike structures thrown across the water like drawbridges over a moat to some little kingdom.

Vermont which is known as the "Covered Bridge State" to many, surprises some by being only fifth in number of bridges, with one hundred and twenty-one covered bridges at present. Vermont's interest in caring for her bridges, however, is possibly first. Pennsylvania has the most, with three hundred and ninety; Ohio is second with three hundred and forty-nine; Indiana and Oregon follow closely behind. At least one covered bridge a week vanishes from the American landscape or rots unattended in the shadow of a new concrete structure, but a few are still being constructed!

Although Connecticut has only three covered bridges left, the Housatonic River alone had eighteen fine examples, each marking a community of mills that has since grown into a riverside town. Connecticut was proud of its bridges, particularly because the two most famous names in bridge engineering, Theodore Burr and Ithiel Town were born there. But ambitious men of those days spread their work in far places: although Burr and Town designed hundreds of covered bridges in almost every state, Connecticut never had more than fifty.

The reasons for covering bridges varied with the builder, but they had primarily to do with strengthening the structure and making the wood season properly and last longer. The more romantic reason for making the bridge appear like a barn, so horses would not shy at the running water, is doubtful. But it adds to the rich lore that surrounds the old landmarks. It fooled two inebriated men of Bennington, Vermont, so the story goes. They approached the bridge there, and thought they had come to their own barn. Dismounting and unhitching their animal so it could go to its stall, they soon found their

71

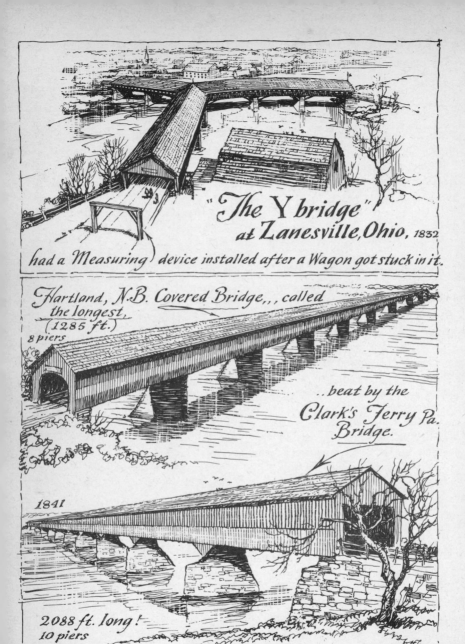

"The Y bridge" at Lanesville, Ohio, 1832 had a Measuring device installed after a Wagon got stuck in it.

Hartland, N.B. Covered Bridge,,, called the longest, (1285 ft.) 8 piers

..beat by the Clark's Ferry Pa. Bridge.

1841

2088 ft. long! 10 piers

Unusual Covered Bridges

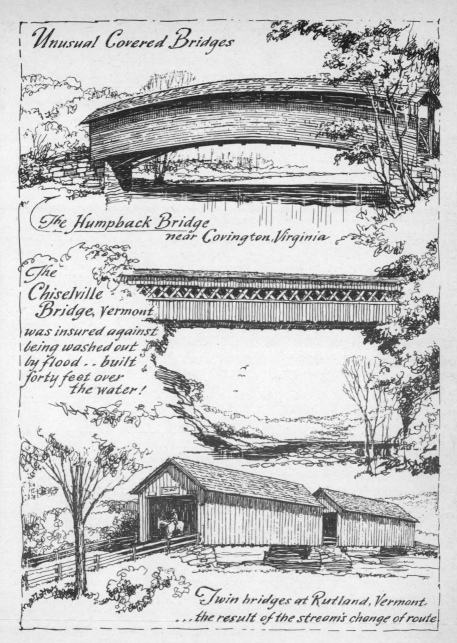

The Humpback Bridge near Covington, Virginia

The Chiselville Bridge, Vermont was insured against being washed out by flood .. built forty feet over the water!

Twin bridges at Rutland, Vermont ... the result of the stream's change of route

mistake but lost their horse and had to pull their wagon by foot the rest of the way home.

The closing in of a bridge to make it appear like a barn must have had its merits when drovers passed through with their cattle, for cows led easily into the welcome shade. In fact they often refused to leave and needed urging to come out the other end. Meat was delivered on the hoof in the old days, and often one herd of cattle made up for a week of poor business at the toll bridge. A yearly account book of the Toll Bridge between Windsor, Vermont, and Cornish, New Hampshire, shows about seventeen thousand creatures passing through on their way to Boston. Drovers sometimes came through with mixed herds and the tolls then became so complicated that an itemized bill sometimes had to be made up and sent by post. One story tells of a farmer who included two hundred turkeys in his drove from Dedham to Boston: when he reached a bridge, the toll-taker refused to let the turkeys pass because turkeys were not listed on the bridge's toll-board.

A reason for covering a bridge, which has seldom been mentioned, is for appearances. When toll-collecting was entirely a private enterprise, there was something distinct about using a covered structure which seemed to make a bridge passage worth that much more. The added expense would seem unnecessary today, but bridges were often built for resale and they were therefore made to look as attractive as possible.

Many people think that covered bridges are the oldest kind of American bridge, but the first covered bridges appeared after 1800. Charles Wilson Peale, well known for his paintings of Washington, wrote an "Essay on Building Wooden Bridges" in 1797, in which he stated, "It has been advised to make roofs to cover bridges and some of them are to be constructed in America." Timothy Palmer is given the credit for being the builder of the first American covered bridge, at least the only one of which there is some accurate record. That bridge was over the Delaware at Easton, Pennsylvania, and it bore the words on its portal: "T. Palmer, Bldr., 1805."

Earliest America knew no bridges at all. There were simply stepping stones for foot travelers and fording-places for horses and riders. Stepping stones were once so much a part of every village road that rope handrails were often supplied by the village, and the repair and replacement of stones was included in road-maker's contracts. Bridges were built adjacent to fords so that when a bridge washed out, a crossing by wading or swimming would not be too far away from the road. Over fifty years ago, travelers by wagon often ignored small bridges entirely during summer but drove off the road and crossed at the nearby fording-places so their horses could get a drink at the same time. And twenty-five years ago, these same fording-places were used for washing automobiles. Today small bridges and fording-places are

The first Outdoor Advertising was on Covered bridges

BURNS & TAYLOR CLOTHIERS

C. A. Rennacker CLOTHIER
33-41 ASYLUM ST. HARTFORD

at Windsor, Conn
over the
Farmington River

at Bridgeville, N.Y. 1817

WICOMA — THE PERFECT CURE

the Medicine Bridge
at Lexington, Virginia

JUST SUITS TOBACCO

"Just suits" tobacco.
Over East Creek, Rutland, Vt.

5¢ Coca-Cola — Delicious and Refreshing — Coca-Cola

Coca-Cola bridge
at Portland, Pennsylvania

75

Stepping Stones were the Road-builder's responsibility -

The Bridge at the Ford came next ..

(to the ford)

Always good for a Stop and a drink for Dobbin.

only rural memories: motor cars zoom over cement culverts and dried-up streams where a stop at the brook was once a pleasant event of any journey.

Some of America's oldest stone bridges still remain. Even many of the obsolete zigzag or "Z-Bridges" which are now bypassed by new structures, still stand. These erratic bridges which stump the experts with their reason for being, were mostly centered around the old National Road in Ohio, where they persisted into the automobile age, piling up more wrecks than their picturesqueness was ever worth. Some say they were designed in shape of a "Z" in memory of pioneer Ebenezer Zane. Others say it was a method of making horses break from a gallop into a walk while crossing a bridge. Another theory is that they were designed by the builders of the National Road to discourage a new forty-foot freight wagon which was being considered at the time. A forty-foot wagon with horses pulling it, of course, could not maneuver such a crooked bridge without getting caught between the zigzag walls. Whatever the idea of the bridge was, the builders forgot winter when they designed it for snow piled up within the crooked roadway and even sleds avoided Z-bridges during snowy weather.

ONE MIGHT wonder why the inventory of early American implements does not include some sort of road snowplow. The reason is that snow was never a threat but rather was it an asset to the average road traffic of a hundred years ago. The last thing an old-time farmer would think of doing would be to clear snow from his road, for he had looked forward all year to the time that he could use snow-covered roads for hauling his heavier loads. At the first sign of snow, sleds of all sorts emerged from the barns, and the hauling of timber or stones began without the bother of bogged wheels or the slough of mud. When the snow finally began to melt, the farmer put away his sleds and he forgot about further heavy transportation.

The only winter road equipment of yesterday was a machine to preserve snow. The "Vermont snow-roller" packed snow down to make it smooth and to make it last longer. Consisting of wooden rollers and a platform on top for rock-ballast, this machine is now probably one of the scarcest pieces of New England Americana. Shelburne Museum in Vermont unearthed what they believed to be one of the last snow-rollers. But even this book might bring to light others hidden away in barns, that were hitherto listed as unexplainable farm equipment.

Sleds were once used both with or without snow, wherever there was any heavy hauling job to be done. There were "stone boats" for moving rocks, lumber-sleds for logs, pungs for general farm use and innumerable sleighs for pleasure and personal transportation. Children tobogganned down grassy

Z-Bridge

New Concord, Ohio. 1828

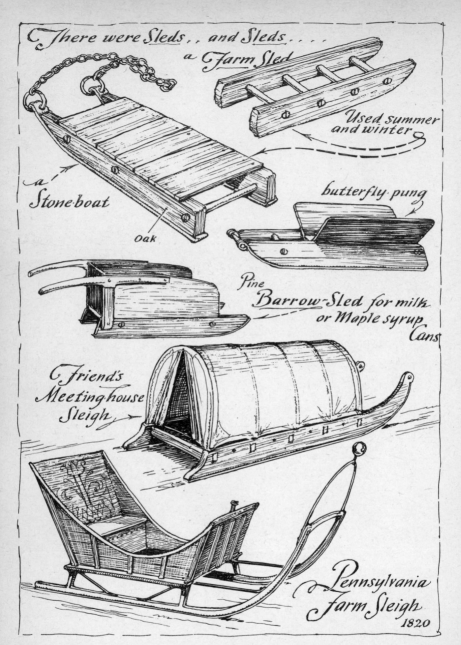

There were Sleds.. and Sleds....

a Farm Sled

Used summer and winter

a Stone·boat

Oak

butterfly·pung

Pine Barrow-Sled for milk or Maple syrup Cans

Friend's Meeting house Sleigh

Pennsylvania Farm Sleigh

1820

78

slopes during the summer almost as easily as they did on snow during the winter. If a farmer of the past could return today, his first reaction might be wonder at the disappearance of sleds from the rural scene.

Far preceding the invention of the wheel, and the crudest vehicle known, the sled is also the fastest. In 1954 a sled was chosen as a rocket-propelled land machine which reached the record of 632 miles an hour. The object was to determine how much acceleration a man can stand leaping from a jet plane. After discarding wheeled vehicles as being too frail, a sled that could have done service in any farmer's barn was built to make the final test. Sleds were

Rocks

Vermont Snow-Roller

.. it didn't Clear the Snow.. it Packed it

Summer-sledding in South Carolina

also the fastest thing in the world of a hundred years ago, for the sail-sled or iceboat was doing sixty miles an hour when railroad trains were still in the creeping stage. One of the most popular Currier and Ives prints shows iceboats racing trains up and down the Hudson River, where there were ice-yachting clubs with memberships in the thousands. The milding winters and disappearance of suitable ice is now making the iceboat a thing of the past, but its record average speed in excess of 145 miles an hour (faster than that of a sports car), testifies to the efficiency of the sled principle. Oddly enough, Oliver Booth who built the first ice yacht in 1790 at Poughkeepsie, New York, predicted that he had designed what would become the fastest land vehicle in the world.

My book, *American Barns and Covered Bridges* drew many critical letters about a drawing that showed two horses hauling a load of sixteen cords of wood on a jack-sled. They said it was impossible and that the drawing looked ridiculous. The drawing, however, was traced from an actual photograph in a New York State *Conservationist Magazine,* and it seems still not to be the record. So here is a later tracing from the October, 1954, issue of the same magazine, showing an even greater load. "The load contains 157 logs," reads the account, "and the number of feet in the load was 35 markets." A market is a lumbering term meaning a log 16 inches in diameter at the small end and thirteen feet long, so 35 markets would be equal to one gigantic log 455 feet long. "The logs were hauled five miles," the account continues, "where this picture was posed with fifteen men besides Mr. Ingram the reinsman, seated or standing on top of the load."

The first
Ice Yacht
was a box on runners

13 ft.

Thirteen feet above the sled, 16 men aboard!

TURNPIKES

MANY of our busiest modern highways are called turnpikes without those who travel upon them really knowing how the word "turnpike" originated. A turnpike was a turnstile for wagons with horses or oxen: originally it was an actual pike or pole that turned on an axle to admit travelers after a toll had been paid. Long Island's Union Turnpike, Jericho Turnpike, and all the other "turnpikes" throughout the country are names carried over from the past when a pike turned or raised to admit travelers past the tollhouse. There is hardly an old highway today that was not at one time a privately owned turnpike built for profit. The turnpike age was a colorful part of Americana of which little is remembered: it brought towns closer, and made a few men rich, but, more important, it laid out the economic landscape in a manner that has continued for over a hundred years.

Turnpike roads were roads built by a company that charged admission, payable at tollgates along the way. The rates were variable and the laws inconsistent until the early part of the nineteenth century when rates were regulated by turnpike commissioners who were appointed by the House of Representatives.

Here is a typical Connecticut act of the year 1836:

> The several turnpike companies in this state are authorized to collect the following toll at each gate where a toll is allowed by law;
>> For each wagon, body not hung on springs, drawn by one horse, *six cents and three mills.*
>> For each four wheeled pleasure carriage, drawn by one horse, *eight cents.*
>> For each wagon for transporting loads, two beasts, *twelve cents and five mills;* for each additional beast, *three cents.*
>> If such wagons are empty, half the sums aforesaid.

The section following reads,

> "No turnpike company will collect these tolls unless voting the following exemptions to wit: all persons travelling to or returning from a meeting of public worship, if such a meeting is held in the adjoining town; also persons going to or returning from military service." It further stated that persons traveling less than four miles on ordinary farming business, were also exempt from paying the turnpike toll.

The turnpike tolls were at one time so complicated that the collector almost had to have mathematical training to survive. A percentage was added during the winter, yet sleighs went by for a cent less than wagons. A mule paid the same as a horse, but two oxen paid the same price as one horse. To add to com-

Spear or "pike" used on Long Island's Hempstead Turnpike

Tollgate in Norfolk, Conn Greenwoods Turnpike

plications, the width of wagon tires regulated the admission to turnpikes because narrow wheels caused ruts, while wide wheels helped to flatten the road. Some of the wagon-wheel tires were six and eight inches wide, designed to save tolls, and even wide detachable tires were invented to put over thin wheels. There were scouts who watched out for those who removed their "cut-rate" detachable tires when out of sight of the toll-collector, and a fine of one extra toll was collected for that offense. Those who knew the countryside, often made "shunpike" trails around tollhouses, some of which eventually became permanent roads parallel to the turnpike. The Lancaster-Philadelphia Turnpike had nine tollgates in all, spaced about seven miles apart, so there was plenty of room for shunpike activity in the Pennsylvania hills.

Before 1800 about seventy-five turnpike companies had incorporated and were selling shares. The Philadelphia and Lancaster Turnpike Road Company was the first, and its road was built at a cost of $465,000, all of which was provided by individual investors. Within an hour after its subscription books were open, the company had sold over twenty thousand dollars worth of shares at thirteen dollars a share. The road was completed in 1806 at a cost of about $7,500 a mile. The success of this road paved the way for a new era in American business, and short connecting private turnpikes sprang up all over the Pennsylvanian landscape. The Dauphin Turnpike in Pennsylvania reported that in one year (and before the snows of winter closed its gates) sixteen thousand people had passed by.

In 1800, the first turnpike in Long Island opened for farm wagons, but within a short time there were many pleasure turnpikes leading to the nearby beaches and mountain resorts. The Jamaica and Rockaway Turnpikes in New York were used every day during the summer season, and were filled with carriages that came across on the ferry from Manhattan to Brooklyn.

The success of the turnpike business, however, was short-lived. Public interest leaned toward the railroads, which were more dependable than muddy turnpikes, and private road fortunes disappeared overnight when the government took an active interest in turnpike business. The first road built with funds from the National Treasury was the Great National Pike, once called the Cumberland Road which linked Cumberland, Maryland, to Vandalia, Illinois. It was built in sections from 1806 to 1840, and was hailed as the first link in bringing the east and the west together. The National Pike was America's first great highway and as one historian put it, ". . . the road looked more like the avenue of a great city than a trail through the country."

A full team pulling a Conestoga wagon stretched out to sixty feet in length, so turnpike traffic must have been a problem, even if the going was slow. The custom of leading a horse from the left, and the convenience of having the teamster's seat also on the left side of the wagon, is why turnpike wagons traveled to the right of the road; because of that, Americans started driving on the right side of the road.

The early 1900's found turnpikes taken over by the automobile which unfortunately could not go through mud-puddles or around stumps in the road as horse-drawn vehicles could. Early touring cars that ventured on highways were therefore equipped with spades and wooden planks.

Peru, Vermont 1913
"10 cents a mile but bring your own mud-planks."

The complaints of the automobile trade and the failure to improve turn-pikes sounded the final death knell of private turnpikes. Typical of this problem was the Peru Turnpike of Vermont which was listed as a "must" in the "Ideal Tour" for vacationers through the Berkshires and White Mountains. The Rutland *Herald* reported that it had 150 water bars on five miles of road. Tourists carried their own "mud-planks" to bridge these handicaps and then complained bitterly at the fifty-cents' admission fee which amounted to ten cents a mile. After five years of such complaints by the automobile tourist trade, the Peru Turnpike gave up, and the road became a free thoroughfare.

BICYCLES

ONE MIGHT presume that the hard-top road was the result of the automobile age, yet the first such roads were designed for the sole use of bicycles. While automobiles were still struggling along back-country dirt roads, bicycle clubs had organized into powerful groups who sponsored hard-top roads, even paying for building them. The League of American Wheelmen was the first organized group of American voters to demand better roads. In fact, many members included demands that automobiles be barred from improved bicycle roads, or at least placed on adjacent gravel road sections.

At the end of the 1800's the bicycle had become a national issue. People were spending over a hundred dollars for a bicycle, often keeping four or five in one household at a time when a fine buggy could be bought for fifty dollars.

Hundreds of factories were turning out over a million bicycles a year and many businesses had to gear themselves to the bicycle-age or fail. The clothing industry featured bicycle-wear for everyday street use. Hat manufacturers, after appealing to Congress to make every cyclist buy two hats with every bicycle, settled on making cycling caps for men and women. Whole church sermons were devoted to the bicycle. "Whether bicycle riding on Sunday is sinful or not," the *Wheelman* of 1882 read, "depends upon the spirit and associations of the ride." Amelia Bloomer designed the famous trousers for women cyclers that shook the fashion world, and businessmen came to work in bicycle pants and stockings.

Whatever the social and economic influences of the bicycle were, its influence toward scientific road-building is still felt in present-day America, although we who regard the bicycle as a toy, find it hard to believe.

ROAD SIGNS

MILESTONES were the first road signs. Even highway inns failed to take advantage of road advertising and they depended entirely upon one sign on the building to advise the traveler of their trade, often no more than the name of the proprietor. Covered bridges were first to gather advertising matter. Perhaps they were prompted by their necessary toll-list and "Walk your horse" signs, but by the middle of the 1800's the inside cross-timbers of covered bridges were filled with posters. Kickapoo Indian Oil, Kendall's Spavin Cure, Dr. Flint's Powders and other familiar trade names of the time, printed strips to fit standard eight-by-eight bridge timbers, and out of the shadows of old bridge portals were born the first attempts at American national advertising.

Although we all know that Bull Durham Tobacco, along with Mail Pouch, Carter's Little Liver Pills, Fletcher's (*children cry for it*) Castoria, Bromo-Seltzer, and Miles Laboratories gained first recognition from the sides of old barns, it is strange that there are no historical records left of this fact. "While the writer has been with the concern for twenty years," writes the head of one of the aforementioned companies, "he has no information concerning painting on barns done by this Company in the past. He therefore talked to our advertising manager who came with the Company forty years ago. He neither can recall anything about signs on barns. We regret our inability to give you information about an important milestone in our business and in the industry of American advertising."

Because barn advertisements were first painted to be seen from the trains, and covered bridges existed before established railroads, it may be said that covered bridge signs came first. When bridge signs lost popularity to the thousands of barns that could be seen by train travelers, the entrance walls of covered bridges became place for only local announcements and circus posters. The few ancient theatrical posters that were protected from weather by the wide portals of old covered bridges and are still intact against the sun and snows of a hundred years, have now become collector's prizes.

Perhaps you have noticed during drives through the country, chalked arrows and other strange markings on telephone poles. This is the language of the circus, put there by an advance man to inform and direct the performers

Sharp turn, big hill.
Good Coffee

to their next destination. A double arrow means a sharp curve, other lines warn of steep hills, detours, unfriendly policemen, or even good restaurants. Even the performers are seldom aware of it, but these chalked signs are things handed down from the time when the circus was frowned upon, had to hold secret performances, and was guided by such signs to avoid unfriendly towns. Connecticut's Acts and Laws of 1784 ruled that no one "shall exhibit on any Public Stage or Place, any Tricks, Plays, Juggling or Feats of uncommon dexterity, tending to no good and useful Purposes, but tending to collect together Numbers of Spectators and gratify vain or useless Curiosity." Theatrical exhibitions continued to be against the law, even a hundred years ago in many places, and circuses were often named in the Statutes as "public nuisances."

America's barns were painted red because the only paint available at first was that which the farmer could mix himself, using home-grown linseed oil and red oxide of iron. But many of the first paint companies were formed by the sign-painters themselves who painted barns for the privilege of including an advertising sign on the highway or railroad side of the barn. They were armed with printed stories of how paint preserves wood, and sometimes had one half of their wagon painted while the other side was left bare to prove their point. The bare side of course, was in terrible condition with the help of shotgun "wormholes" and "termite" gougings by the sign-painter himself. The real truth is that the oldest barns in America are usually the unpainted ones while those with many coats of paint have long since disappeared. This is no condemnation of paint, which is necessary for most of today's lumber. It is proof of the well-seasoned virgin timber of yesterday which was allowed to breathe and dry by contact with the weather, and lasted longer without the use of paint that might have sealed moisture inside.

The itinerant sign-painter was one of the little-sung artists of America who left a lasting impression on the lore of the countryside. Actually, many of our first portrait and landscape artists were traveling sign-painters. Edward Hicks whose "Peaceable Kingdom" has become a masterpiece of primitive American art, lettered mileposts for country roads, did signs for taverns and painted a gigantic Washington Crossing the Delaware for a covered bridge at McKonkey's Ferry. Thomas Hicks of the same family did coach-painting and commercial signs, yet left his name behind as a master at portraits.

The traveling sign-painter of a few years ago was seldom a recognized artist, but he, too, left an impression behind. With his office in his hat and no more equipment than he could hold in a small box, people got to know his work and waited till the next time he came through town for the signs. Many sign-painters were as much dependent on a bottle which was usually evident in their paintbox, as they were upon their paints. Yet many were quite the opposite, spending their spare time denouncing drink in signs on abandoned houses and barns. Some were evangelists who, instead of signing their own names to a piece of work, added a line or two from the Bible. When they had nothing to do for the moment, and a high rock made an inviting medium, they could never resist putting the word of the Lord there too. You could hardly venture out of town without seeing "Jesus Saves," "The Love of the Lord is Good,"

Signs of Civilization

or whole passages from the Psalms written on whatever flat surface the landscape offered. One such rock on which was painted "Stop and Repent," rolled downhill during a spring freshet and ended near the middle of the road near Brattleboro, Vermont. Wagons drove around it for a long while, thinking it was a religious monument placed there for some good reason, until it was finally removed by the State.

During the winter when the going was hard, the traveling sign-painter spent his time doing cardboard signs which he later carried with him and sold on the road. "In God we trust, all others Cash" was a close favorite over "We'll crank your car and hold your baby, but we won't cash checks and we don't mean maybe." Country banks were always a prospect for ready-made road-warning signs such as "Go slow and see our country; go fast and see our jail," "Drive Slow—you might meet another fool," or "Sharp turn ahead— prepare to meet your Maker."

Not long ago when people traveled slowly enough to read road-signs, most cities had billboards at both ends of town that featured a short history of the

a Spreader Sign

place. A tire manufacturer took over this idea and made road-signs in the shape of big history books; they educated the traveler, however, more than they sold tires. In a small village, the sign-painter could always contract as many shopkeepers as there were letters in the name of the town and put up a "spreader-sign." Spreader-signs had one large letter on top of each advertisement so that when seen in a line on the highway by the oncoming traveler, they spelled out the name of the town. Many an eastern sign-painter contracted and collected for a spreader-sign only to find that hard western ground is too stubborn to dig pole-holes into. There was nothing to do then but to place the signs in dents in the ground and get out of town before the wind blew them down. Spreader-signs are still to be seen in the western part of the United States, but the idea took hold in a different version in 1926, when the Burma Shave Company put up a series of signs on U. S. Highway 65 near Lakeville, Minnesota. It said, "Cheer up . . . face . . . The war . . . is over" But it soon changed to a rhymed, "Hinky-dinky . . . Parley-Voo . . . Cheer up face . . . The war . . . is through." Now, the Burma Shave Company changes its seven thousand sets of rhymed signs once a year and finds its idea has become an accepted part of the American highway landscape.

Free water for Autoists

When Taverns where built to be. Taverns, and looked like Taverns...

The King of Prussia 1709
Pennsylvania

Burnham Tavern
Machias, Maine
1770

The Rising Sun
Fredericksburg, Va
1760

Munford Inn,
Munfordsville, Ky
built of 30 ft. walnut logs, 1800

Salem Tavern, Winston-Salem, N.C.
1772

The Jolly Post-Boy, Frankford, Pa.
1749

Munroe Tavern 1695
Lexington, Mass.

Fraunce's Tavern N.Y.C.

ROADSIDE taverns are by no means disappearing from the American land-scape, but their changes are worthy of noting here. Like the big city which has reached a limit in size and has now begun to spread out into the suburbs and countryside, the tavern, too, has reached its limit. Dispersed over the country as motels and houses made into small hotels with "tourist accomodations," the average rural tavern of today is a far cry from that of a hundred years ago.

In the beginning, the tavern was built to be a tavern. It was the club and meeting-place for those who lived nearby and the place where news always arrived first. The first tavern-keepers were nominated yearly. Connecticut's "Acts and Laws" of 1780 read that "the Civil Authority, Selectmen, Constables and Grand-jury-men in the respective Towns of this State, shall some time in the month of January annually, nominate the Person or Persons whom they, or the major Part of them think fit and suitable to keep an House or Houses of public Entertainment in the said Town for the ensuing year." Inn-keepers were not always nominated, however, though they were always looked upon as village officials; to get a license they had to be "passed by select-men, and possessed of a comfortable estate." The tavern-keeper's duties were many, and stiff fines were levied from their cash bond for infractions. For example, the tavern-keeper had to "post the names of tavern-haunters on his door" and refuse drink to those men who were judged by the authorities to be tipplers and idlers at the bar.

In the 1800's when road information became a part of most almanacs, the innkeepers themselves were known more than any actual names of their inns. In fact, they were listed in the following manner:

You will notice that Dedham and Attleborough have two inns listed. In such cases where the coach might have hurried past one of the inns, a flag or a ball signal was used to stop it for a passenger or mail. Although the Ameri-canism "ballin' the jack" and "highballin' through" which is used to indicate a no-stop expresslike speed, is credited to railroad language, it first came from stagecoach slang. A large metal ball was lowered to the ground as a signal to stop, but a "high-ball" hoisted to the top of the post meant "go right on." The same signal continued on into the railroad age and trains "highballed" past no-passenger stations.

In the 1800's a tavern always had its flagpole and religiously displayed the national flag. The American flag and flagpole is unfortunately a characteristic

to the principal towns, from Boston, with names of the innkeepers and distances in miles.

Boston to Newport.

Roxbury	Whiting	8
Dedham	Ames and Gay	3
	Ellis	3
Walpole	Polly	7
Wrentham	Hall	6
Attleborough	Hatch	5
	Newell	4
Rehoboth	Carpenter	7
Warren	Cole	8
Bristol	Bourn	4
Ferry-house	Pearse	2
Portsmouth	Congden	7
Newport		5
		69 miles

The HIGH BALL

of the vanishing landscape, when almost every country home had its flagpole and every household had an American flag.

Stagecoach-drivers were like truck-drivers of today in finding the best and cheapest place to eat along the highway. Wherever there was an authorized traveler's inn, there was also a teamster's and drover's tavern close by, noted for its food and drink. Our modern version, the "highway diner" has likewise contributed roadside hospitality to commercial drivers and has elevated itself to a top position with the traveler too. Beginning as a "lunch wagon" or "dining car," the first diners were built from discarded trolley-cars. Even now, the proportions and windows and curved roof of trolley-car anatomy have prevailed in the most expensive and plush models. It is odd that long after trolley-cars have disappeared from the American scene, their architecture should live on as restaurants.

The modern American architect has had no fair trial at designing public taverns. There are those who specialize in "Old English" or "Rathskeller" façades and the result is too often a cartoon-effect of overseas tavern architecture. So-called "good taste" was not the most desirable quality in early tavern design, but the vigorous and functional simplicity that suggested the

93

purpose of the building, made it as individual in the American landscape, as the church.

In every big city you will find one or two untouched taverns where people go to enjoy escape from modern neon restlessness. The fact that such places are old is not as important as that the effects of age have been allowed to stay. Friendliness and comfort have not yet caught up with the modern cleanliness and smartness of our new highway architecture, and there are still those who would trade chromium brightness for the dim restfulness of the past.

The first one

COUNTRY CHURCHES

As you approach any unspoiled American village, the first heart-warming sight is the tall white spire of a church. A little slower to go the way of the covered bridge and the little red schoolhouse, the little old-fashioned church remains one of the last symbols of a vanished landscape. Occasionally you will find a fine example left intact, but too often looking out of place in the city that has grown up around it, like an ancient tombstone or monument to the past.

By the early 1800's the American meeting house had reached a degree of architectural elegance unsurpassed by other buildings of that time. As boxlike

94

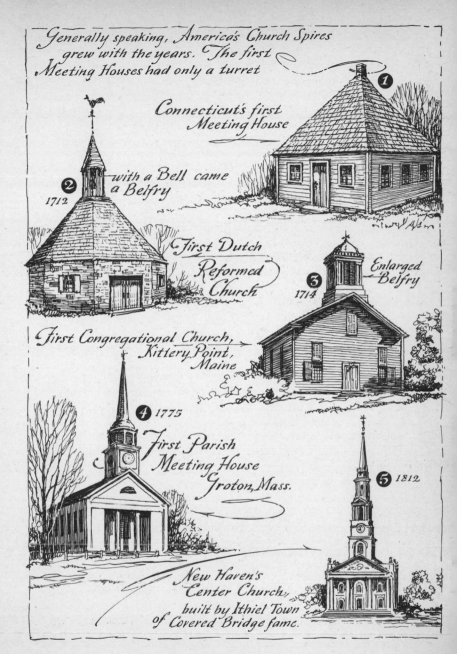

Generally speaking, America's Church Spires grew with the years. The first Meeting Houses had only a turret

1 Connecticut's first Meeting House

2 1712 with a Bell came a Belfry

First Dutch Reformed Church

3 1714 Enlarged Belfry

First Congregational Church, Kittery Point, Maine

4 1775 First Parish Meeting House Groton, Mass.

5 1812

New Haven's Center Church, built by Ithiel Town of Covered Bridge fame.

and plain as they may have been, they were always classic in their portrayal of their reason for being. At first there was no attempt to copy Europe's monumental stone churches and there was no ornamentation to remind one of the English Church which the Puritans had left behind. But when bells were cast on this side of the sea and a belfry or steeple was built to house them, the tall spire became part of the structure. It took about a hundred years for the steeple to mature in the architecture of the American church, and although there were some early church spires, generally speaking they became bulkier and taller as the eighteenth century progressed.

Before the middle of the century, the vogue for classic formalism swept the country and soon no church was complete without wooden reproductions of stone Greek columns. Yet the quietness and severity of early American design was too striking to be hidden by any ponderous revival architecture. The stark lines and direct white spire of the country church have always been one of the outstanding features of the American landscape.

Many of our old churches have spires and towers that were later additions, built when the pioneer's aversion to "dressing up divine and glorious truths" was tempered by the invasion of classic architecture. The Society of Friends were content with the clean shapes of plain structures; the only major difference between their meeting house and their home was size. They criticized church spires as being poles to hang a fancy weathervane on. "But the weathercock," explained the builders of steeples, "was a church symbol from the beginning." The origin of the weathercock has been hidden in the ages because the earliest weathercocks were made of light wood and have long since decayed and disappeared. The story has it that Pope Nicholas I in the middle of the ninth century ordained that a figure of a cock should surmount the top of every church throughout Christendom to remind the people how Jesus said Peter would deny Him at cockcrow. The Nativity and the Resurrection occurred near cockcrow, and an ancient superstition predicted that when the

Spires like silent fingers of Faith

cock ceased to crow, the Day of Judgment will be at hand. From these religious symbols, our weathercock evolved, devised to turn with the wind.

There are countless oddities in church steeples, such as the one of the First Presbyterian Church in Port Gibson, Mississippi. Atop its spire there is a twelve-foot hand, pointing toward the heavens. It commemorates a gesture of Rev. Zebulon Butler who founded the church in 1807. In Marion, Massachusetts, the Captain's Meeting House was built with a three-faced clock so only a blank wall faced those towns which had refused to contribute to its construction. The First Congregational Church in Wellfleet, Massachusetts, has the only town clock in the world that strikes "ship's time."

The carriage shed has now almost entirely disappeared. All early church buildings had sheds to protect carriages from rain or snow, but they have been left to rot in an almost deliberate manner. Churchgoers often have to walk in the rain from cars parked blocks away, yet yesterday the protective roof of a carriage shed was always close by the entrance. Even modern gasoline filling stations are usually uncovered: both your gasoline tank opening and the attendant are exposed to the downpour of rain. The old-fashioned carriage shed idea, it seems, would be a welcome and inexpensive piece of architecture, even in this automobile age.

Wherever you see abandoned country churches you will usually find abandoned farms too. The failure of farming and the disintegration of small communities often go hand-in-hand. If we look deeper, as Representative Clifford Hope of Kansas suggests, ". . . it may be that the people's spirit and the failure of their faith brings on the failure and neglect of their land."

The small rural church is much more than an architectural feature of the countryside, and as a vital force of American life its disappearance would be no trivial matter. Politicians argue that churches, like schools, must be built larger to accommodate cities rather than to restore small outlying country churches. There are sixty thousand more churches today anyway, they point

97

out, than there were thirty years ago. But another fact is that twenty-five thousand small country churches have closed their doors during that time and big city churches have taken over their remaining parishes. Many farmers would no more go to a big-city church than they would call in a big-city doctor when they felt sick, so countless country people who are unwilling or unable to make the trip to the city, have stopped going to church altogether. Old-time church suppers and meetings that were once elements of rural culture are losing in popularity or, as some insist, have lost their dignity and meaning by becoming bingo parties.

Yet the country church continues to be a major American force, as stubborn as its white spire against the changing landscape. If skyscrapers are monuments to American industry, the small rural church is symbolic of our heritage. Such symbols preserved by a longing tethered to the past, whether it be a distant church spire, a gracious bend in an old road or just a reverence for trees and the old ways of farm life, become more important as they vanish. But if some good things are destined to be only memories, we can still be thankful that though they have disappeared, the memory has remained.

Cock weathervane,
New Brick Church,
Boston

a little Gallery of Sketches from the Vanishing Landscape

Barns are at their best in Winter.
The snow blankets the unheated parts, yet melts over the Stalls, from Animal Heat

...or breaks the back of the weak barn

In Summer, the Barn becomes closer to the landscape...

the old barns blending with the landscape as only weathering wood can

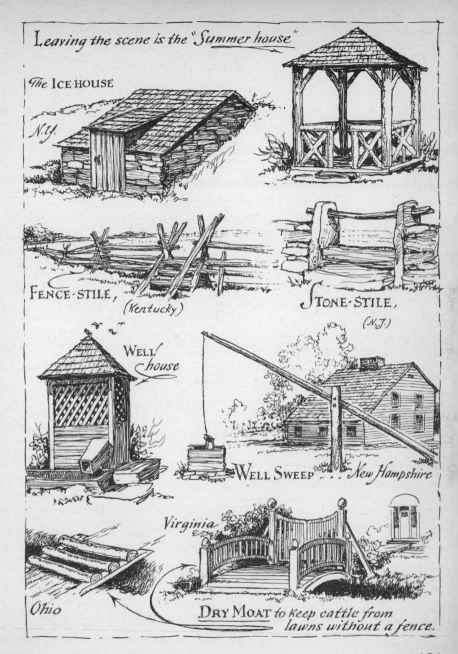

Leaving the scene is the "Summer house"

The ICE-HOUSE
N.Y.

FENCE-STILE,
(Kentucky)

STONE-STILE,
(N.J.)

WELL house

WELL SWEEP .... New Hampshire

Virginia

Ohio

DRY MOAT to keep cattle from
lawns without a fence.

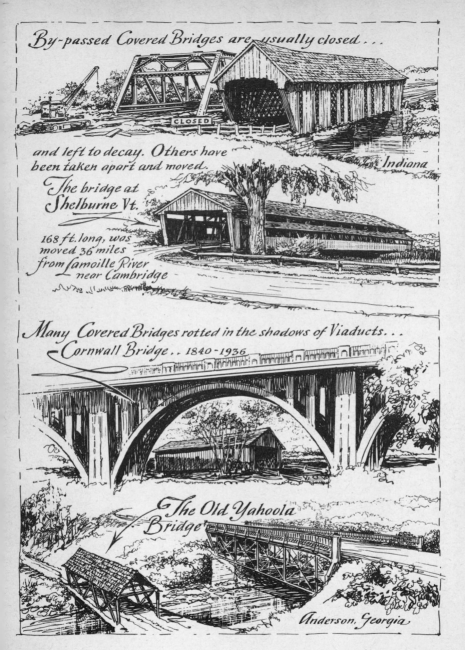

By-passed Covered Bridges are usually closed . . .

and left to decay. Others have been taken apart and moved.

Indiana

The bridge at Shelburne Vt.

168 ft. long, was moved 36 miles from Lamoille River near Cambridge

Many Covered Bridges rotted in the shadows of Viaducts . . . Cornwall Bridge . . 1840-1936

The Old Yahoola Bridge

Anderson, Georgia

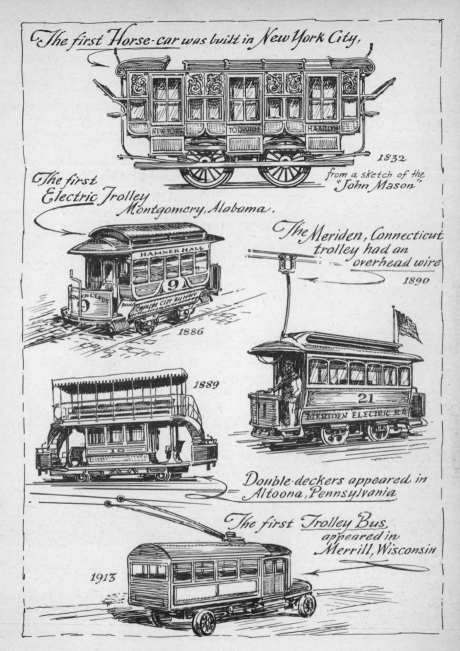

The first Horse-car was built in New York City,

1832
from a sketch of the "John Mason"

NEW YORK · YORKVILLE · HAARLEM

The first Electric Trolley Montgomery, Alabama.

HAMNER HALL
9
UNION DEPOT
CAPITOL CITY RAILWAY
1886

The Meriden, Connecticut trolley had an overhead wire
1890

21
MERIDEN ELECTRIC R.R.

1889
10

Double-deckers appeared in Altoona, Pennsylvania

The first Trolley Bus, appeared in Merrill, Wisconsin

1913

103

Early American

Church design

varied....

The Round Church in Richmond, Vermont

First Presbyterian, Port Gibson...1859

1812

Octagonal Church at Burlington N.J.

Santa Fé's San Miguel 1710

Virginia...1690

The Blackwater Presbyterian (like BARNS)

1796

Frankford, Delaware

Meeting House, South Wardsboro, Vermont

DOORWAYS *as individual as signatures* . . . .

Exeter N.H.

Peacham, Vermont

Providence R.I.

FENCES *were Unique too* . . .

Fairfield, Conn.

Cape Cod

W. Dennis, Mass.

Even a man's Stone Fence *bespoke him* ➝

LAID   THROWN   CHINKED

Good-bye to BOG MEADOWS ..

and DITCHES ..

and DRAINAGE PONDS ..

..... they have no place in the changing landscape.

106

Bog meadows, ditches, drainage ponds and forest-growth are now evil words to the cleared landscape --- but they once helped to prevent floods in flash storms.

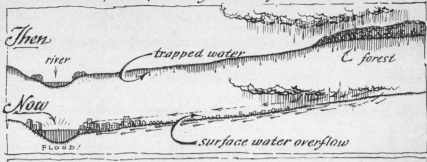

Then
river — trapped water — forest

Now
FLOOD! — surface water overflow

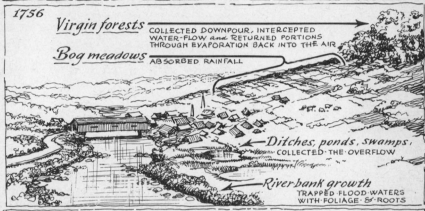

1756

Virgin forests COLLECTED DOWNPOUR, INTERCEPTED WATER-FLOW and RETURNED PORTIONS THROUGH EVAPORATION BACK INTO THE AIR

Bog meadows ABSORBED RAINFALL

Ditches, ponds, swamps, COLLECTED THE OVERFLOW

River bank growth TRAPPED FLOOD-WATERS WITH FOLIAGE & ROOTS

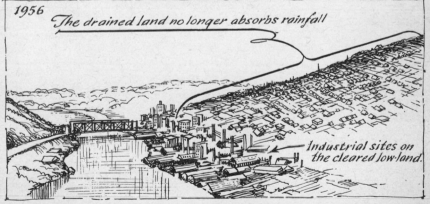

1956

The drained land no longer absorbs rainfall

Industrial sites on the cleared low-land.

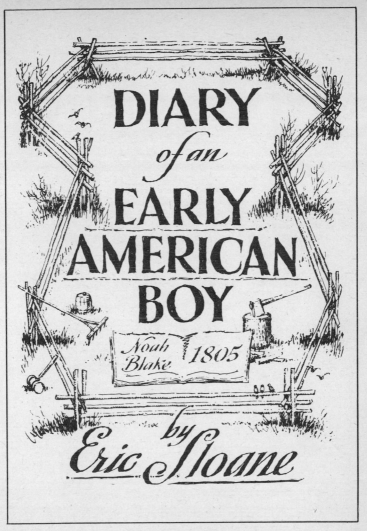

DIARY *of an* EARLY AMERICAN BOY

Noah Blake 1805

by Eric Sloane

This diary, complete with Sloane's famous pen-and-ink drawings, gives unusual insight into what it was like to grow up in 19th century America. (5¼″ x 8″)

$5.95 / 32100-6

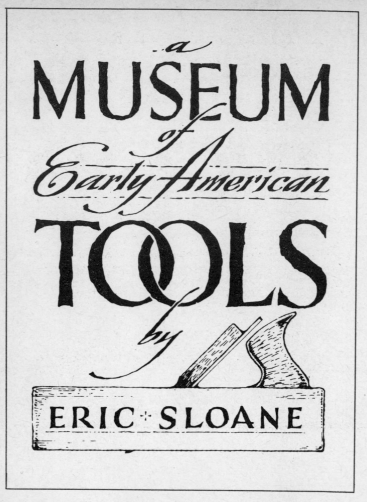

a MUSEUM of Early American TOOLS

by ERIC·SLOANE

This uniquely illustrated study of craftsmen
in Colonial America discusses early tools and artifacts
used by wheelwrights, coopers, blacksmiths,
and many other proud and individualistic craftsmen
of the pre-industrial age. (5¼″ x 8″)

$6.95 / 33216-4